It Seemed Like a Bad Idea at the Time

THE WORST TV SHOWS IN HISTORY
AND OTHER THINGS I WROTE

BRUCE VILANCH

CHICAGO
REVIEW
PRESS

Published by Chicago Review Press Incorporated
814 North Franklin Street
Chicago, Illinois 60610
ISBN 978-0-914091-92-9

Library of Congress Cataloging-in-Publication Data
Names: Vilanch, Bruce, author.
Title: It seemed like a bad idea at the time : the worst TV shows in
    history and other things I wrote / Bruce Vilanch.
Description: Chicago : Chicago Review Press, 2025. | Includes index. |
    Summary: "Emmy Award winner Bruce Vilanch is known as a go-to comedy
    writer for award shows, sitcoms, and top-heavy variety specials, but he
    has also been responsible for quite a few of the worst shows ever
    made-legendarily bad productions. From The Star Wars Holiday Special to
    Rob Lowe dancing with Snow White at the Oscars, Vilanch reveals how he
    helped create some of the worst moments in television—and beyond"—
    Provided by publisher.
Identifiers: LCCN 2024037658 (print) | LCCN 2024037659 (ebook) | ISBN
    9780914091929 (cloth) | ISBN 9780915864669 (epub) | ISBN 9780915864492
    (pdf)
Subjects: LCSH: Television programs—United States. | Television
    broadcasting—United States—Anecdotes. | Vilanch, Bruce. | Television
    comedy writers—United States—Biography. | LCGFT: Television criticism
    and reviews. | Autobiographies.
Classification: LCC PN1992.3.U5 V56 2025 (print) | LCC PN1992.3.U5
    (ebook) | DDC 791.45/750973—dc23/eng/20241010
LC record available at https://lccn.loc.gov/2024037658
LC ebook record available at https://lccn.loc.gov/2024037659

All images are from the author's collection

Typesetting: Jonathan Hahn

Printed in the United States of America
5 4 3 2 1

To Dolores Greenberg Friedman—the OM

Contents

Introduction. 1

1 *The Star Wars Holiday Special* (1978)
Or, at Least We Didn't Have Jar Jar Binks 3

2 *The Paul Lynde Halloween Special* (1976)
Or, at Least We Had the Real Wicked Witch 33

3 *The Brady Bunch Hour* (1976–1977)
Or, at Least We Didn't Have Cousin Oliver 61

4 *The Ice Pirates* (1984)
Or, at Least the Space Herpe Didn't Have Lines 83

5 *Can't Stop the Music* (1980)
Or, at Least Disco Was Already Dead 103

6 *Platinum* (1978)
Or, at Least a Chandelier Didn't Fall and a Helicopter
Didn't Crash. .121

7 *Three/Comedy Tonight* (1994)
Or, at Least This Didn't Make Joe Allen's Wall, Either . . 145

8 *The Look of the Year* (1998)
Or, at Least the Sushi Was Fresh. 151

9 *Charo* (1976) and *Henne* (1991)
Or, at Least It Wasn't *The Love Boat* (or We Would Have
Had Charo and Carol Channing in the Same Show) . .157

10 Oscar! Oscar! (1989)
Or, at Least Nobody Sued . . . Oh, Wait a Minute,
Somebody Did 169

Coda: Or, at Least They Were the Worst. 183

Acknowledgments 189

Index 191

Introduction

Warning: Everything in this book happened before there were podcasts. I know. It may take some of you a moment to recover. But here's the interesting rub—this book happened *because* of podcasts.

During COVID, podcasts spread almost as fast as the virus, and I got invited to be on a bunch of them. Almost all of them were hosted by people in their twenties and thirties, on lockdown, bored, surfing the internet twenty hours a day. Inevitably, they encountered some of my output that has been hanging onto the web like spiders waiting for you flies. Some of them were TV variety shows committed long before these young 'uns were born, and naturally, when they took a look at them, their first question was always "How did this thing happen?"

A deeper dive usually revealed my name, and they came to me for an answer. And here it is, in your hands. A book about how I helped create the worst shows in television—and lived.

Creating the worst shows in television of course spilled over into helping create the worst shows in other media as well, and I have not spared you the details. Movies, Broadway musicals, revues . . . sooner or later I wound up getting involved in more turkeys than the Osmonds at Thanksgiving.

Oddly enough, the Osmonds show I wrote for, *Donny & Marie* (1976–1979), was a success, and even though most everything on TV during that period comes across as cringeworthy when viewed today, they didn't bother people too much back then. I've worked on other things that were *hits*, believe it or not. Twenty-five Oscar shows, some of them getting me Emmys, helped me live down the reputation of my first Oscarcast, an experience described in exquisite detail toward the end of these adventures.

I've also had my hand in some of the most important successes of some very talented people—but all that will have to run in place until the next book. My mission here is to answer the timeless question *Why?* Why did these . . . things . . . turn out the way they did?

No one sets out to do a bad show. They just happen. Nothing in this book justifies any of what was done. It just describes, in jaw-dropping succession, how it happened. And if you want to add an *SH* to the front of the *IT* word, that could be one all-encompassing explanation. But the real stories are much more fun.

1

The Star Wars Holiday Special (1978)

Or, at Least We Didn't Have Jar Jar Binks

It was morning in L.A. and you could hear the birds coughing.

That observation didn't originate with me. It was famously said by comedian Bob Hope. But it didn't originate with him, either. Very little of what he said actually did. He had a fleet of very funny and consistently sour writers.

Most people who write jokes for other people have a sour tang to them. They work for wildly competitive, ego-driven creatures, and they are under constant pressure to deliver. Even hookers have it easier, and many of them make more money. Of course, if you're in the Writers Guild, which is the professional union of screen and TV writers, you at least have a dental plan. It's not as good a dental plan as the actors have, but then, actors need their teeth. Writers can be toothless hags.

I worked for Hope—he was always known out here as Hope. If you are a little too young to remember Hope, you should know that he was the biggest full-service radio/movie/television star and stand-up comic of the previous century. He was Seinfeld and Kimmel and Will Ferrell in one brilliant package, better known than most of the heads of state who got to play golf with him. There is a famous story about a network head being interrupted at a high-level meeting by an aide who breaks in and says, "The pope is dead." The network guy turns ashen and slumps over the table.

"My God," says the aide, "I had no idea you had such reverence for the pope."

The guy lifts up his head. "Oh, sorry. I thought you said Hope."

I freelanced on and off for Hope for a time in the '70s. When we met, he said, "The last time I saw tits that big on a blonde was Jayne Mansfield." From that day on, he called me Mansfield.*

I would get calls from exotic locales like Indonesia. "Hey, Mansfield, it's Hope. Whaddya know about this Dewi Sukarno broad?"† Some men still do talk that way. Really, they still do.

Back to my morning. The phone was ringing—did I mention it was 1978, when phones still rang? Well, this one was ringing, even louder than the birds were coughing, but I'd learned long ago not to answer it in the morning, if ever. If there's a family emergency in the East or Midwest, where you most likely came from, or you've been nominated for a major award, you'll know before the sun comes up. Otherwise, from then till noon it's just people bound to ruin your day in one way or another. And it was—my agent. With an offer.

---

* Jayne Mansfield: an extremely blonde comedic actress, developed (you should pardon the expression) by 20th Century-Fox to threaten Marilyn Monroe, should the blonde bombshell step out of line. Mansfield, who was no dumb blonde, had a following of her own and delivered some witty performances in *The Girl Can't Help It* (1956) and *Will Success Spoil Rock Hunter?* (1957), in which she effortlessly parodied Monroe. She had a vivid tabloid presence with her muscleman husband Mickey Hargitay, and they are the parents of Mariska Hargitay of *Law & Order: SVU*.
† Dewi Sukarno: a glamorous Japanese woman who, between 1962 and 1967, was the First Lady of Indonesia and a tabloid sensation, probably because how many Japanese First Ladies of Indonesia do you know?

Normally a good thing. Let me take a moment here to explain how this one wasn't.

He said four words: STAR WARS HOLIDAY SPECIAL.

It seemed like a bad idea at the time.

But I ignored that. Actually, it was no worse than any other bad idea that was being floated around for a pre-Thanksgiving holiday show.

It would air at the midpoint of what was known as the November sweeps, one of the four months of the year when the TV networks' viewership ratings would be used to set commercial advertising rates for the following year. Networks piled on their biggest event programming during these periods. And the current period was, after all, in 1978. This was the era of bad TV specials.

Actually, it was the tail end of the era. Cable television had appeared only a few years before and basically begun to put the variety show format out of business. By the early '80s, If you loved a certain performer, you'd no longer have to wait for them to show up on Ed Sullivan or Carol Burnett or Dean Martin. They were available 24-7 on any number of cable channels. If your taste ran to younger, less conventional performers, like Madonna or Michael Jackson, you could see them all day and all night on MTV. Well, you could see Michael once MTV got woke.*

Comedians who used to spend hours wondering whether the people from Kraft cheese would allow them to tell a certain joke no longer had to worry. HBO wouldn't give a shit. And in 1975 NBC, taking one of those leaps of faith a corporation occasionally indulges in, had programmed a live variety show late Saturday night that was allowed to get away with a lot more than a prime-time variety show could. They even called the cast the Not Ready for Prime Time Players.

---

* When it first went on the air, MTV famously did not show Black artists. Hard to believe but true. Their theory, if I remember it correctly, was that they were a rock and pop station, not rhythm & blues. Michael crossed the color line. And erased it.

Liberated from many of the old "standards and practices," audiences began to find the prime-time variety shows stodgy and out of touch. You couldn't compete with freewheeling comedy by doing comedy that had brakes on it.

To put the final nail in the coffin, the traditional vaudeville/Broadway/music hall/radio/socko/boffo entertainers just weren't happening anymore. A full-service variety star was no longer a necessity. You could do one thing well and make an empire out of it. Singing, dancing, comedy. You didn't need to be a triple threat. One big threat was all you needed.

So the people who classically carried a weekly variety show on their shoulders—Jackie Gleason, Dinah Shore, Sid Caesar, etc.—morphed into teams like Sonny & Cher, Rowan & Martin, Donny & Marie, Tony Orlando & Dawn, down to the very last successful prime-time variety series, *Barbara Mandrell & the Mandrell Sisters* (1980–1982). Variety itself would reappear decades later disguised as competition shows,* but during those few decades before the resurrection, the genre stretched out on its deathbed, represented by awards shows, tributes, and specials, in which I was a player till the last gasp.

There were also magic shows. I wrote a few of them, two of which were hosted by those noted magicians Tony Randall and George Burns. There were beauty pageants, one of them held in Japan, hosted by George Hamilton, featuring the Pointer Sisters and actual magician David Copperfield—not doing magic but judging beautiful models, and loaning George Hamilton his traveling tanning bed. There were shows I didn't write that featured Wayne Newton in various exotic locales . . . Raquel Welch being shot out of a cannon and then singing "California Dreamin'" while walking along the banks of the Seine . . . Wonder Woman, Lynda Carter herself, onstage in Vegas with many boy dancers . . . Joey and Dad, being sex bomb Joey Heatherton

---

* Like *American Idol, America's Got Talent, The Voice, So You Think You Can Yodel,* and so forth.

and her father, Ray Heatherton, known to all of us who grew up in New York as the Merry Mailman . . . the Sonny comedy hour, with Sonny but not Cher . . .

I mean, there were lots of strange shows and I'm sorry I didn't get to do them all. Really, I am. Because I know that with the correct chemical additives, they were a lot of fun to do. I did, legendarily, get to do some of them, and I want to share the wonderful, stoned, giddy thrill of creating a small sampling of what have been called by many critics, bloggers, podcasters, sponsors, and some of my relatives the worst shows in the history of television.

Nobody sets out to write the worst shows in the history of television. Look, they don't *seem* like the worst shows when you're writing them. Actually, you're having a good time. You know that what you're writing is inconsequential, a passing entertainment. Not, in anyone's mind, designed for the ages. This is not Eugene O'Neill. In the depth of his despair, he never sat down to write a two-spot for Donny and Marie. He was too busy tearing another gut-wrenching tale of family woe from the dark portals of his heart, in between rinsing out the shot glasses.

When you write something for variety television, you don't have the burden of greatness taking up residence on your shoulders. And you *are* getting paid, unlike Eugene O'Neill, who understood the maxim all playwrights understand—the theater is a great place to make a killing, but a lousy place to make a living. In TV you can make either, or enough so that you can walk away and exercise your inner O'Neill. If you have one. And you feel like letting it out to play. Not everyone does, especially with the dazzling array of substances we have at our disposal to keep our inner O'Neills at bay.

But that doesn't explain how you write the worst shows in TV history. As I mentioned earlier, it starts with a call from your agent. And in this case, these four words:

STAR WARS HOLIDAY SPECIAL.

Why was there a *Star Wars* holiday special, you might ask? It's a question that has echoed through the wormholes of time since it was first asked, probably not by me, but I certainly was in the original cast of people who asked it. The reason was—and I know you may have read something about this somewhere else, but I was there, and this is how I remember it:

Star Wars had burst upon the galaxy in the summer of 1977, which also happened to be the Summer of Sam,* the summer of a power outage that threw much of the northeast United States into the stone age for a few days, and probably the summer of a few dozen other things that rattled people's nerves. Once power was restored, they flocked to the movies, and to one movie in particular that, from the moment it opened, was a blockbuster. A combination of old-school Republic Pictures serials, the kind kids went to see on Saturdays, and high-tech sci-fi fantasy filled with time warps, chatty robots, and other gadgets, the story was also furnished with several classic gambits.

There was an accidental hero, an unassuming farmer unknowingly born to greatness and forced to step onto his preordained path. There were forces of the light and of the dark. There was a damsel in distress. There was a villain with no face dressed entirely in black. There was Jungian angst filtered through Joseph Campbell and Frank Herbert. And there were creatures. Scary, lovable, slimy, cuddly, terrifying, in many colors and languages, although they all seemed to understand English. It was a great big theme park ride, with just enough of each thing to appeal to almost every sort of audience.

You know all this, of course, but you may not have been old enough—or even alive yet—to know what happened when *Star Wars* exploded into the zeitgeist.

In the movie business, it was a signal that the kids who had grown up watching cheap science fiction on TV and in B movies

* The Son of Sam was the serial killer of the moment, and his moment lasted for years.

had found the toolbox with which they could make serious, big-scale, big-bucks megamovies that dared touch on big themes. As a result, these grown-up kids went and made the most iconic movie since *The Wizard of Oz* nearly forty years earlier. You know that now, even if you weren't here then, because the iconography became part of global culture and has never stopped being there, like Santa Claus, the Easter Bunny, and the Tooth Fairy. An alarmingly large fringe group still treats it as a quasi-religion, filled with sacred, untouchable beliefs.

As the months rolled along, pop culture's newest icon rumbled forward and picked up speed. But in the summer of 1978, it paused.

The film had been in release for a year. Other films had come along to capture the public's imagination. *Close Encounters of the Third Kind*, a space adventure of a different kind, was one. The upcoming Superman movie starring Christopher Reeve, which would kick off the comic book superhero craze, was another. *Grease*, which brought the '50s nostalgia of popular sitcoms *Happy Days* and *Laverne & Shirley* to the wide screen with a Broadway twist, created some of its own icons.

Up in Marin County, California, where latter-day hippies sprawled out along the slopes of Mount Tamalpais in tempting yoga positions, the next installment in what was now envisioned as the *Star Wars* saga, *The Empire Strikes Back*, was in lengthy preproduction at George Lucas's Skywalker Ranch. It wouldn't start shooting till March 1979, and would not be in theaters until 1980. The pop culture audience, being slightly fickler than the crowd that fills Carnegie Hall to hear two-hundred-year-old scherzos, needed to have their pump primed for the next journey to a galaxy far, far away.

Either someone at CBS, or someone at ILM, or somebody in the IRA, or on the IRT—depends on which version you've heard—suggested producing some sort of *Star Wars* spectacle for TV to keep the franchise bubbling on the burner of public awareness until the second installment was released. (Remember, this all happened forty years ago and nobody took serious notes. And there was no worldwide-internetweb or social media to keep people irresponsible.)

It's just as likely the brainstorm came from CBS as from the *Star Wars* people. For the network, it would be a chance to "young up" the schedule with a name-brand movie-ish event. I tend to believe that they approached Lucasfilm with the idea of a special. In those pre-global-village days, the Lucasfolk would've seen it as an easy way to keep *Star Wars* in the air, and a no-brainer of a promotional tool.

But then came what I am convinced was the epic misunderstanding. I don't think George, or his people, understood what a network variety special *was*. I believe they thought that this was going to be some kind of original musical based on one of the stories George had spun for his galaxy of characters. I don't think network variety specials were really in their wheelhouse, or on their flight deck, to put it in galactic terms. If George had watched some of the stuff that was out there, he never would have consented. Jefferson Starship, that great iconic San Francisco band, most likely would not be spotted jamming at the quinceañera of Princess Amidala of Naboo. And yet, they were, sort of . . .

But I'm getting ahead of myself—because I wanted to mention the other epic misunderstanding. Although today it is a given that *Star Wars* caused the Earth to move closer to the sun, at the time of its release, a lot of people didn't take the movie too seriously. At the Writers Guild screening I attended, one Oscar-winning scribe of my acquaintance blinked out into the daylight and asked me, "What did we just see?"

This may be sacrilege to some of you, but a large chunk of humanity considered *Star Wars* a high-tech summer time-killer, full of clunky moments and those cinematic wipes that used to show up in B movies to keep the action going. They weren't overly impressed by anything in the movie, except maybe John Williams's Wagnerian score and some of the technical effects. The pop culture effect of *Star Wars* was, like that of *Jaws* before it, undeniable. But there was nothing like the pseudo-religious frenzy that eventually attached itself to the canon. That was for the next generation to create, after they had a few more chapters of the saga under their belt and time to study them, frame by frame, on their VCRs.

Given this hindsight, it might be hard to recognize that at the time, *The Star Wars Holiday Special* was itself something of a joke idea. If it had been the thing George originally envisioned, it might have gone on to be a joyous season perennial, to be trotted out along with the Bing Crosby–David Bowie duet on "Little Drummer Boy" that routinely shows up between Thanksgiving and Kwanzaa. But, as I think you know, it wasn't that thing.

The one meeting I remember having with George and the other writers was cordial but serious. However, I have to take a tiny break here to bring up some colorful facts. First, if we'd known that forty years later we'd still be talking about this show, all of us might have paid closer attention. Second, it was 1978. There were a lot of chemical additives circulating. I've joked about this so much—I'm fond of saying that Carrie Fisher and I were snorting the Sweet'N Low in the coffee room—that I now find learned treatises stating that "Vilanch, who admits to copious drug abuse," etc. That is a gross exaggeration. The old maxim: "If you remember the '60s or the '70s, you weren't there"—it holds true. Everybody, or almost everybody of a certain generation—Osmonds excepted—was somewhat baked some of the time. Mine was not a copious indulgence. The shows I worked on made the opposite look entirely possible, but that was not the reality.

Now back to George and that serious meeting. He told us he had ten *Star Wars* stories written, six of which he intended to film. He had worked up what we call a bible, which is the story, or saga in this case, from beginning to end. Interestingly, the first *Star Wars* movie was part four of the story, which everyone now knows, but which at the time struck us as one of the more bizarre ideas ever pitched, topping even *Howard the Duck*. However, it was not as bizarre as the story he wanted us to tell.

The four non-movie stories he had in his head were tangential to the saga—think of the latter-day entries *Solo* and *Rogue One*. Three of them had been committed to other media, and the last one was his idea for our show.

Curiously, it revolved around the Wookiees.* Now then—the first thing you notice about the Wookiees is that, like anything in the *Star Wars* galaxy, their name is spelled with two or three consecutive vowels or sometimes consonants or sometimes both. This is not unlike Hawaiian, though in the latter tongue every word also contains a *k*. Pretty much every creature or place in *Star Wars* is like this, or if their names are short, they're abbreviated versions of the real names, which are several dozen letters long and could pass for entire conversations in Hawaiian.

The second thing you notice about the Wookiees is that they speak no English, nor any other language in our current universe, known or unknown. They don't speak at all, as we know it. They grunt, and for emphasis, they yowl. They sound a lot like fat people having orgasms. Trust me, I know. They *understand* English, of course, like every other creature in the galaxy far, far away. They just refuse to speak it, like certain shopkeepers in Paris.

In the *Star Wars* movies, a lot of characters speak a lot of languages that are not English. No, not Klingon—you've got the wrong franchise. Their words are often translated in subtitles. But in 1978, on network television, that was an impossibility.† CBS was very firm

---

* Wookiees: huge hairy upright creatures whose faces strongly resemble Yorkshire terriers. Chewbacca, the bandolero-wearing warrior who flits around the galaxy with Han Solo, is everyone's starter Wookiee.

† It was all but unheard of at the movies, too. Foreign-language films were still being shown in two versions—the original with subtitles and a dubbed version. Woody Allen had a hilarious time taking a Japanese monster movie and dubbing it into bad English. It's called *What's Up, Tiger Lily?* (1966), and if the woke police haven't

on this point. The audience wouldn't sit there and read subtitles. So either the Wookiees did everything in mime, or some English-speaking characters had to appear alongside them to translate what they were saying. And if you were going to introduce a character like that, it might as well be a guest star.

The guest star was by then an intrinsic part of every variety program. It hadn't always been that way. With the exception of some splashy all-star faux events, like the special celebrating Ford Motor's fiftieth anniversary, the memorable early specials simply showcased some simply brilliant performers doing what they do simply brilliantly. Fred Astaire's shows were legendary, and all he needed was the girl to dance with, and she didn't even have to be famous. Noël Coward and Mary Martin just got out there and did Noël Coward and Mary Martin.* Barbra Streisand placed herself in Bergdorf Goodman and the Philadelphia Museum and Central Park.

Specials were, well, special. When you had to deliver a variety program every week, though, things were different. It was widely acknowledged that such bravura talents as Danny Kaye, Judy Garland, and Julie Andrews could not do a different one-man show each week, so high-caliber help was recruited. But for one night only, one singular sensation was all that was required.

As specials became more commonplace, especially as a way of boosting ratings during those sweeps I mentioned earlier, networks began stocking them with guest stars, like the musical comedy equivalent of an Irwin Allen disaster movie. It wasn't unusual to see a show toplined

---

crushed it beneath their boots, it exists somewhere. In context, you are still allowed to laugh while watching it.

* Noël Coward and Mary Martin: two of the greatest stage stars of the last century. He wrote, directed, and headlined in his own comedies, as well as doing a nightclub act and winning one of the early Oscars for his movie about Britain through the years, *Cavalcade* (1933). She went from being Broadway's darling to TV's Peter Pan. Offstage, she was the mother of Larry Hagman—J. R. Ewing on the nighttime soap *Dallas*—which deserves an entire other footnote.

by one star and supported by several others, each doing their specialty then pairing with the star.

It also wasn't unusual to see guest stars who happened to be the stars of other shows on the network. Called cross-plugging, it was common practice. It has a not-so-distant relative who is still alive today. Have you ever spent an evening in Chicago on NBC care of Dick Wolf, with a story that starts with *Med*, continues on *PD*, and ends with *Fire*? I thought so. In sitcom land, one memorable night decades ago there was a hurricane in Miami that tracked through *The Golden Girls*, *Empty Nest*, and *Nurses*. Hurricane Saturday is more remembered than *Nurses* altogether.

There was even a recurring form of cross-plugging that was a literal Star Wars special. Called *Battle of the Network Stars* (1976–1988), it pitted actors from different series against each other in bizarro athletic competitions. Charlene Tilton wielding a shot put, trying not to accidentally take out Webster. If you think *The Masked Singer* is weird, you must check out the *Battle*.

All this is by way of explaining how all of these performers who would be much more at home anyplace but Tatooine wound up on a television show starring a family of creatures you hope would not sneak up on you while you were glamping.

George's story presented us with plenty of opportunities for guest stars who could also serve as translators. It seems that Chewbacca, the *capo di tutti* Wookiee, is on his way home to celebrate Life Day, the big-deal holiday on the Wookiee planet, Kashyyyk. Gesundheit! And aloha and mahalo! George had high hopes, or perhaps he was being funny, it was hard to tell, of Life Day being absorbed into the culture like so many other Stars Wars elements. This was not to be, and our show may have had something to do with that.

But George hasn't given up, even though fans have created a *Star Wars* holiday of their own, May the Fourth (be with you). Nevertheless, he persists. There was a mention of Life Day on the first season of

The Mandalorian in 2019, and the following year there was an entirely new *Star Wars* holiday special starring LEGO characters, including a LEGO Daisy Ridley who looked a lot like Rosie O'Donnell, that was all *about* Life Day, so it ain't over till it's over. And remember, everything here is a long time ago and far, far away.

So Chewie is racing home in the *Millennium Falcon* with his traveling partner, Han Solo. This hardy duo is being pursued relentlessly by imperial stormtroopers in very uncomfortable molded white plastic uniforms that make them all look like late-model Ford Fusions. It will take them a while to get home, and there will be several commercial breaks—excuse me, interruptions in the narrative.

Meanwhile, back at the old Kashyyyk homestead, Chewie's family is busily making preparations for his return and the holiday. Well, Mrs. Chewie is busy. Grandpa and the kid are just slacking off. Mrs. Chewie, whose name is actually Mallatobuck, called Malla for short, is bumping pots like crazy, so many furry faces to feed. The kid, named Lumpawarrump, sometimes known as Lumpawaroo (but only in Australia) and called Lumpy by any nearby being who actually can articulate the word, is all over the place, doing tightrope walks on the banister (it's a tree house, so there is jeopardy), running around with a low screech, and breaking things. His grandfather, a small but mighty silverback Wookiee with a faintly feral grin, is making model X-wings out of perhaps Popsicle sticks as he relaxes in his easy chair. His name is Attichitcuk. So as not to be confused with a leader of the Mongol hordes, he is called Itchy. (Although the Mongol may have been called that on occasion, but only by one of his dozen wives, the mouthy one, and only because she was probably itchy, too. Gesundheit again.)

Itchy and Lumpy bond over a hologram, sort of, being done by people who, as I recall, came down from Canada as part of the nascent Cirque du Soleil. They appear in miniature on a coffiee (Wookiee spelling) table, summoned up by the silverback, and they do an acrobatic routine to some tinkly music, which captivates Lumpy.

This tender domestic scene, replete with chirping birds and light cello music, is played out with no dialogue and lots of hand-waving, grunting, stern expressions of disapproval, and pointing at things. It's like a silent movie without the title cards.

Malla, who has been wistfully hugging a framed photo of Chewie— she is very dainty for a such a gigantic individual—is clearly missing him and tries to scare up some information on his whereabouts. In a galaxy far, far away there evidently are no cell phones, but there is a computer on which a Wookiee can bash out a message to the diaspora. Must have that big dialing pad that you see a lot of in Boca Raton.

So Malla rings up Luke Skywalker, who is in his home repair shop screwing around, assisted by R2-D2, on what looks like somebody's mechanical arm. It seems a droid is getting a tune-up. In the first human voice we have heard since Harrison Ford's explanation of how he was ferrying Chewie home for Life Day (accompanied by grunts and growls from Chewie), Luke says he hasn't heard from the boys and they're presumably on said way home and—wait, are they overdue? More grunts and groans.

This one-sided conversation could go on till the commercial break, but the droid patient on the table has a slight stroke. White smoke begins billowing out of several of his ports, which could mean that he has chosen a new pope but probably doesn't, so Luke must do some quick thinking. The call is therefore ended. Suspense hangs in the air.

How the audience is faring is anyone's guess. With the exception of brief appearances by two *Star Wars* icons, it's a dumb show (as in, no words) about the Wookiees. The entertainment portion so far has been strictly on the level of an Ed Sullivan Swiss bell-ringing act.* It's time for a human guest star.

---

* Ed Sullivan, famous for introducing the Beatles to America on network TV, had a lot of old-school vaudeville acts on his show in between the big stars and much-loved comics. Acrobats, close-up magicians, ventriloquists, and, yes, acts in which a

Enter Art Carney.* A legendary second banana, he jumped into the role of intergalactic Tupperware salesman Saun Dann, mild-mannered shopkeeper and secret member of the Rebel Alliance. Malla dials him up to see what he knows and he gives her the wink that Han and Chewie are indeed on their way home. But he has a lot more 'splainin' to do, so he will drop in on the tree house later on to clear up the rest of the plot. There is just so much you can do with mime and one-sided conversations on TV screens. And, network thinking goes, it can't hurt to have a big, comfortable, likeable star in this galaxy of geeks and gawks and gigabytes.

While waiting for Saun's arrival (it's saun as in sauna, by the way) as well as the arrival of, well, you just never know how many things are going to show up at a holiday open tree house, Malla sets about concocting her Life Day feast. Throughout Kashyyyk, housewookiees are peeling and spatchcocking, and Malla seems to be one of the more adventurous hostesses, as she seeks advice from her TV cooking guru, the Julia Child of the cosmos, Chef Gormaanda. To be fair to George, this may have been our invention. The name certainly smacks more of us than him. We added the requisite vowels just to fool him. But the character was a great excuse for, what else, guest star #2! Harvey Korman.†

---

family done up in Alpine attire wheeled out a table of bells on which they played tunes, note by excruciating note.

* Art Carney, Academy Award winner for his touching performance in *Harry & Tonto* (1974), was for most of his career a TV sidekick to Jackie Gleason in the *Honeymooners* sketches and series as Ed Norton, sewer worker. (Not to be confused with Ed Norton, the actor who for many years insisted on being called Edward Norton for just that reason.) In addition to being a sweet man, Carney was a most accomplished player of many roles, including being one-half of the original *Odd Couple* on Broadway in 1965, with Walter Matthau.

† Harvey Korman was a mainstay of *The Carol Burnett Show* (1967–1978), a Jack and Jill of all trades. He played everything from harried husbands to hammy actors to huge, bosomy maternal figures. He was adored and adorable.

Harvey, of course, was no stranger to playing outrageous female characters. On *The Carol Burnett Show* (1967–1978), he is probably most remembered for his immortal portrayal of Mother Marcus, Canoga Falls' premier yenta, on the soap opera parody *As the Stomach Turns*. With voluminous Bob Mackie boobs (a specialty of Bob's), a print dress that looked like it had recently provided shade at a used car dealership, and over six feet of attitude, he walked away with every scene he was in. Our Chef Gormaanda was an alien and not necessarily female, although somewhere on one of her four or seven arms there must have been a tennis bracelet. She certainly had been to the makeup and hair trailer on her home planet. This was an opportunity for Harvey to do some of the stuff that had worked so well for him on *Burnett*.

Many decades later, I was informed by a keyboard warrior that they thought it was disgraceful and racist that Harvey was in blackface. I thought the comment was a joke. I mean . . . the character was an alien, not of this earth . . . humanoid, granted, but still. . . . I remembered that when we shot it, it was purple face, or maybe green face, or maybe green-and-purple face. Something definitely not human. But when I looked at the fourteenth-generation tape this keyboard warrior had most likely looked at, I thought, gee, this is indistinct enough to actually look like blackface. Hoisted on the petard of bad technology! In spite of this heinous oversight, the culture has stubbornly refused to cancel the show.

Controversial half a century later, it was the first specific moment when, if the audience hadn't figured it out already, the *Star Wars* universe and the network variety show universe collided. The sweet little acrobatic hologram and all the plot-establishing were in the *Star Wars* ken, even if the sets looked cheesy compared to the movie. Harvey's routine was from another part of the forest.

We worked on the bit a lot, and no matter what, it remained strained, because it was, after all, a one-joke idea loaded up with sight gags. When Dan Aykroyd did Julia Child on *Saturday Night Live*, there was an idea behind it: suppose Julia Child cut herself on air and bled to death, sloppily, while ignoring the whole thing and proceeding with her script. Our idea was—suppose Julia Child had seven arms. It was a sideshow moment, while Dan's was in the center ring.

By that point in the show, you know a few things. A fairly flat-footed story is going to be interrupted by some performance or other that will or will not relate to what's going on in the tale. It doesn't take long for one of these musical burps to occur, although calling it that is really not fair to the artist who performed it. Here's how it unfolds.

Once the cooking lesson ends, Art Carney arrives bearing Life Day gifts for everyone, along with news of Chewie's impending arrival. There is a lot of grunting, growling, and translating, but before long, Itchy is enjoying his present, and it's a truly interesting item.

Many years before, I remember reading a science fiction novel, and I didn't read many and only read this one because the person who gave it to me said it was written in the '30s and had something in it I would like. The something was a kind of helmet that you wore and it somehow dug into your brain and took you on whatever sort of trip you wanted to go on. Let's say you wanted to fly. It would make that happen, only without you ever leaving your recliner. It was a dream machine, what would later become known as virtual reality. I, of course, immediately glommed on to the pornographic opportunities it offered. Greater minds than mine went other places. Either George read that book, which I later found out was a minor classic, or great minds do operate on a single track, because he came in with this idea of a virtual reality helmet, which unfortunately we put to work as an opportunity for another performance that looked like a hologram. Part of the reason it did was that the helmet was on Itchy, a horniee Wookiee, and the fantasy it plugged into was Cher.

Until it wasn't. The idea was for Cher to do a sexy number that would give the old silverback a shot of testosterone, or his species' equivalent. But Cher begged off, not feeling up to it, or maybe just not feeling like being a fetish object for an old Wookiee. Not that a thing like that would ever get in her way. She's fearless and fierce.

Also fearless and fierce was her replacement, the sublime Diahann Carroll. Shepherded by one of our producers, Joe Layton, the brilliant director-choreographer who had made her a Broadway star, Diahann poured herself into the costume and assumed a position she had never assumed before—sex siren. She of course was the epitome of elegance in everything she did, yet I know she loved cutting loose in this weird number playing to an audience of one, this thirsty carpet with eyes, ogling her in his dreams.

During a break, I mentioned to her that this was undoubtedly the first instance of an interracial, interspecies romance on network television, and every time I saw her, for decades afterward, I would ask her if she had received that NAACP Image Award that I knew was rightfully hers, or any sort of sci-fi fantasy doctorate from an institution of higher or lower learning. We decided to write a forceful letter to several of them, but never got around to it. She became such an icon of style and taste that even when the special surfaced on the internet, people didn't believe she really was in it.

In subsequent decades, some other keyboard warriors have noted that they felt the number was quasi-pornographic and wondered how we got away with it on a family show. So I looked at it again through the quasi-porno gaze. This was not as difficult as it might seem. It rarely is, for me. Frankly, I don't know how we got away with it. We had a big star and it was a fantasy and she was doing the number to a guy in a gorilla zoot suit. Yet it was always a tease, never meant to be lusty or lewd. And, as noted, some of us were chemically altered. Maybe even the network censor.

The next few hours of the show—OK, minutes, but they seem like hours—involve lots of plot, which means more of the grunting, growling, shrieking, and translating that had mesmerized audiences when it was done by Patty Duke in *The Miracle Worker* but didn't thrill them overly in our show.

A particularly awkward exchange brings forth Carrie Fisher in her basic Princess Leia white dress and Danish pastry hairdo. Carrie, who I met when she was in the chorus of her mother's (Debbie Reynolds, as if you didn't know) Broadway musical triumph, *Irene* (1973–1974), had literally skyrocketed to fame in the first (or fourth, if you are a Lucasyte) film in the *Star Wars* saga. She wasn't thrilled about being on the show, but she had been told that there would be a musical element and she was eager to be a part of it. Desperate, almost. She really wanted to be a singing actress, like her mother, but not like her mother, if you catch my drift.

Carrie already had plenty of edge. (So did Debbie, one of the last of the old-school studio contract players, but she had been trained never to show it.) Carrie wanted Leia to sing, specifically something by Joni Mitchell, maybe with a guitar—in that white dress . . . shades of *The Singing Nun*—but the Mitchell camp wasn't having it. Carrie did wind up singing in the big Life Day finale, but that wasn't exactly what she had in mind. She spent a couple of days mooning around the production office, auditioning various pieces of material and generally hanging out and being very entertaining. We became friends, and I tried to massage something musical into the show for her, but it never was going to happen. Nobody saw Princess Leia as a breakout singing sensation.

In her first appearance on the show, Carrie and C-3PO are chatting via Zoom—OK, it was teleconference back then—with Malla and Art Carney. For some inexplicable reason, Carrie and the robot were shot from a low angle, looking up at, presumably, the TV screen, so there are lots of views of Carrie's throat and chin and her eyes focused on a point somewhere behind and to the north of the audience's head. This is a very low-key, non-warrior moment for Leia, and consequently there wasn't much that Carrie could do with it but be patient and polite while every grunt, squeak, and squawk out of the Wookiee is translated. It's all on point for the story, setting up what is to happen later. Sizzling it isn't.

As I mentioned, the story isn't strong, but it does have a basic throughline: get Daddy home for Christmas. Daddy has to deal with a few obstacles along the way. Almost none of them open up avenues of entertainment and they all rely on the kind of special effects and action that a network variety show was not equipped to provide.

So it's up to the breaks in the narrative to deliver all the amusement. Make way for more holograms. You'd think two would be enough, but we found spots for one more, plus a cartoon and a couple of video inserts.

The video screen at House Chewbacca—a big wall unit—was useful for moving things along. In fact, looking at the show today, it feels a lot like all of those new movies where the entire plot revolves around people staring intently at their cell phones. That really is art limiting life, and the invented word is intentional. Today it doesn't seem at all unusual that everything in the Wookiee household revolves around what they get in their video feeds and the messages they send and receive around the galaxy.

We did manage one boutique moment when, as a diversion, Malla opens her video music box and there is a hologram of Jefferson Starship. Why she would have Jefferson Starship in her video music box collection is an open question. Grace Slick had left the band, so there was no strong female presence for Malla to fan out over. And Malla never struck me as the type who would have gone to San Francisco with flowers in her hair, winding up in a commune in the Haight and later a rehab in Marin, but the Starship was in that box for some reason. We debated it internally for about a minute and moved on to more pressing issues. Like, where were we gonna stick Boba Fett? Could he spring out of that box, too? Of course not. He was too much a part of Lucas World to be a mother's plaything. So he became something that Lumpy pulled up on his televiewer.

Probably half of you know every single fact, fun fact, factoid, fun factoid, and scurrilous rumor about Boba Fett. And probably the other half have never heard of him. He made his introduction on the special and became more famous in subsequent *Star Wars* movies, and the fact that he suffered such a low birth as to first appear on our show has enraged the faithful for decades.

Boba Fett always was meant to have his own storyline and pride of place in the *Star Wars* canon, but for reasons that are only George's to tell, he showed up as a cartoon in our show, with both of his *t*'s proudly on display. Who knew forty years later he would wind up with a deal at Disney+?

We had nothing to do with the cartoon, and the cartoon had nothing to do with us. It was produced by a studio in Canada, and all we had to do was plug in a moment for it to be rolled into the show. Since it was a previous adventure of Chewie and Han, there's a good reason for Lumpy to watch it, because he can see his father and wax nostalgic. I suggested we have Malla watch it and, when Chewie is threatened, have her burst into a Susan Hayward moment of madness and tears, but that got a quick veto.

When we first saw the video, I immediately recognized Boba's voice as that of Don Francks, a Canadian who had starred in a legendary one-night Broadway flop called *Kelly* (1965) but then gone on to appear opposite Petula Clark in the pre-*Godfather* Francis Ford Coppola's movie version of *Finian's Rainbow* (1968). He had a huge Broadway voice. Boba the belter.

Luckily, he didn't have to sing. Although it wouldn't have hurt. The cartoon was widely considered to be the only Lucasian thing in the special, and therefore subsequently became revered.

Watching his father's adventures inspires Lumpy, or so the god of the subtext whispered in my ear, and he gets industrious, coming up with a way to get rid of the imperial stormtroopers who are staging an elaborate bivouac in his house while waiting for Chewie to lumber into their trap. Lumpy's plan is to somehow create a translation device with a voice feature. Two cans, a wire, and Art Carney could have done the trick, but that was another veto. Besides, Art is busy leading the stormtroopers astray in their search of the tree house. I never knew what they were looking for, certainly not Chewie. Where do you hide a ten-foot-tall Wookiee? I'm guessing they were hoping to find Colonel Mustard in the library with a candlestick, but it's never resolved. Meanwhile, Lumpy, device invented, is trying to get a robot to record a voice in stormtrooper language—that would be English—to get the boys to return to base. This provides an excellent opportunity for Harvey Korman to return, this time as a robot, and make a mangle of Lumpy's best intentions.

This is another one-joke bit, but it's light-years better than the Julia Child, because it has an idea, not just a funny costume. The robot is not the newest model and it's having a mechanical breakdown that, because Harvey is playing it, turns into an emotional breakdown as well. He pulls every rabbit out of his deep, deep hat. Tics, sudden speech impediments, complete loss of physical control, instant restoration of all functions followed by slow shutdown, and underneath it all, the understanding that he's losing whatever shreds of dignity he has left each time something goes wrong. And he's bitter about it. It's really a master class, and stuck in the middle of this miasma, it shocks people because it's actually funny and true.

There is just so much you can do when the Wookiees are your lead characters, but one of the things you can do is figure out a way to get the action away from them and let a subplot rule for a minute or twenty. That was the thinking behind one of the more notorious sequences in the special.

The original idea was to have the *Millennium Falcon* stop off on Tatooine, Luke Skywalker's home planet, barren though it be, partially to dodge imperial stormtroopers and partly to refuel, and to have them stumble into the local watering hole for the scum of the universe. We seem to have dropped that idea somewhere along the way, and what remains is, for no discernible reason, a roll-in of things that are happening elsewhere in the galaxy while the Wookiee planet is on lockdown.

The Cantina—and I can hear you humming the *dit dit dit dit ditditt dit* John Williams music as I type—is where all manner of life-forms gather to get soused and let the good times roll. In our version, it is presided over by the incomparable Bea Arthur, in her best Statue of Liberty mode. She is large and in charge and nothing escapes her gimlet gaze.

At the time, Bea was coming off *Maude*, the sitcom hit that she had before *The Golden Girls*, her sitcom megahit and the best possible third act of a life spent making people laugh. The first act had been spent on Broadway, where she was the original Yenta, the matchmaker in *Fiddler on the Roof*, and where she won a Tony in 1966 for playing BFF to the title character of *Mame*, the acid-tongued second or third lady of the American stage Vera Charles. Now ensconced as a bona fide television star, Bea—who had broken through in New York theater circles singing in the marathon off-Broadway production of *The Threepenny Opera*—music by Kurt Weill, lyrics by Bertolt Brecht, *danke schoen* very much—was looking for opportunities to remind people she was a Broadway belter.

So she reacted favorably to jumping onto our show, provided she could blast out a number to the balcony. We knew this would be stretching it, but then the Cantina came to mind. Why not have a human floor show for the aliens? There wasn't much for them to do that they hadn't already done in the movie. They were all sight gags to begin with, and watching them get drunk, fall down, accidentally taser themselves, and pick fights with each other that none of them can win because they can barely move had been adequately covered on the big screen. So they could hover in the background whispering "peas and carrots, carrots and peas" to each other as all the supernumeraries at the Metropolitan Opera do, while Bea played a faux-seduction scene with an amorous alien played by, you'll never believe this, Harvey Korman. Interesting variations on the action include Bea pouring a cocktail into a hole in Harvey's head, as one does when one is serving an alien who drinks through . . . a hole in his head.*

Harvey's hole was haute couture designed especially for him. The rest of the aliens, if my copiously doped memory serves, had to be rustled up from the vaults of science fiction epics gone by. We didn't want to use the same old aliens. Who does, really? George had a whole bunch of new aliens he was about to film for *The Empire Strikes Back*, but we would never get our mitts on those. So the designers went alien shopping, and it seemed like a lot of them came from an alien outlet just off the freeway on the way to Palm Springs. They were aliens with manufacturing defects. Some were not in the best repair. There was the whiff of Elmer's Glue-All about them, and a couple of yellow, fraying pieces of Scotch tape decorating one of them.

And one of them was a dead ringer for a vagina. I wasn't the only one who felt this. Whispers went around the set the first day the aliens appeared. You generally don't want to say anything, but when you run into a vagina doppelgänger, it's cause for comment on the platform. Years later, when we spoke of this, and we did, we were kind.

George has something of a vagina leitmotif running through the *Star Wars* canyon. There's a typo. *Canon.* There always seems to be something that resembles a vajayjay in each of the movies, although deeper research by a scholar in the field is probably required to prove this thesis. The most notable involves Jabba the Hutt, or Jabba Desilijic Tiure, to the initiated. Jabba first appears in episode six of the saga (also known as

---

* Nothing to do with *Star Wars*, but a fun footnote for the wannabe *Jeopardy!* champ: both Bea and Harvey starred in American versions of the cult British sitcom *Fawlty Towers*. Harvey's was known as *Snavely* (1978) while Bea's was called *Amanda's* (1983). They each played the John Cleese role. Both shows had early trips to their glory.

the third one to be released from the first folio), *Return of the Jedi*. He is the huge squat beast with bling resting on a barge in the middle of the desert, picturesquely overlooking the Great Pit of Cartoon, pardon me, another typo, the Great Pit of Carkoon. Carkoon could pass for a vagina, if one ever happened to appear in the middle of a desert. This one swallows up quite a few items, which is a textbook nightmare some people have. It almost gets Jabba, but he is strangled by Carrie, wearing an outfit they wouldn't let Barbara Eden wear on *I Dream of Jeannie*, an image that became a masturbatory fantasy for a generation or two.

So Carkoon is the most outstanding example of vagina placement, except for this one alien who presents himself in the cantina on Tatooine on our show. Naturally, we fell in love with him and affectionately named him Cuntface.

We didn't think Cuntface would make the cut, not once the network censor got a look at him. But the crew at CBS's Standards and Practices, the self-righteous title all the networks gave their scissor-holders, was light-handed compared to their colleagues at the other two behemoths. CBS had, earlier in the decade, executed the great Stalinesque purging of its rural comedy shows—*Hee Haw*, *The Beverly Hillbillies*, *Green Acres*, everything in Mayberry—in favor of the more sophisticated and even edgy *All in the Family*, *The Mary Tyler Moore Show*, *M*A*S*H*, *The Bob Newhart Show*, and more. Still licking their wounds from the battle of *The Smothers Brothers Comedy Hour*,* the network was loath to be viewed as anything but a fertile ground for content creators. So Cuntface's casting passed without comment.

---

* Tommy and Dickie Smothers were a hip, collegiate folk-singing duo who became hosts of a very successful Sunday-night variety show from 1967 to 1969. It became more and more political as the Vietnam era progressed and ran into a lot of censorship problems as the boys became poster children for free speech and the attitudes of the next generation. Unfortunately, they still came in second in their time-period after *Bonanza*, but nothing could beat the adventures of those White boys on the prairie with their Asian American cook, Hop Sing, who did neither. Just cancel this footnote now.

Maybe it was the heat. We were out at the Warner Bros. studio in Burbank, and it was September and the sun was pounding down. Air-conditioning could do just so much when combined with bright lights, heavy costumes and prosthetics, and of course an insufferable amount of standing around waiting for something to happen—the resting face of all productions involving a camera.

Being an alien is something like being Pluto or Goofy or any of those colorful characters at Disneyland. You spend your shift living in a giant head perched atop your shoulders. There are invisible eyeholes built in so you can see where you're going, but not much else. You never speak. Children come up to you and torment you and you have a small vocabulary of gestures you can make your arms use to register surprise, delight, or love, but sometimes the kids just wanna fuck with you. I had a short friend who played Dopey, of the Snow White clan, for years, and she told me that when the kids got too handsy, she would pull her arms into her costume and spin herself around, as if Dopey had suddenly become a whirling dervish. The arms then became propellers—which, if her aim was good, would whap a kid if he got too close. She said she never got reported for this. She said.

She also said that in the summer months, she routinely passed out while on duty, often face-planting in the middle of an attraction. The heat was just too much. This would get noticed, and an all-points bulletin would go out to an on-deck Dopey, who would race to her location and wave the kids away while medics dragged her behind one of the many barricades that dot the parks.

This was kind of like what was happening on our set. Aliens would drop under the hot lights, spoiling a take. Bea took it in stride, but her wig and drag were pretty warm, too, although not smothering. After a while, it became slow going. And we were losing aliens by the hour.

Each time one of them went down, I would quietly move Cuntface closer to Bea. See, here's a tip if you're ever going to be an extra in a movie or TV show. Stay as close to the star as the bodyguards will allow. You're more likely to make it into the show—and be seen!—the closer you are to the star in the frame of the shot. They're not going to cut much of what the star is doing. So Cuntface got closer and closer to Bea each time some poor unfortunate visitor from Kkakkabally or Yenemmvelt or some other galactic gated community was taken away. Finally, it was just the two of them in the frame, Cuntface and Bea. We were that underpopulated.

Bea had brought in a Brecht-Weill tune to sing. It may have been Brecht-Weill to her, but for our show, it was vile Brecht. "The Alabama Song." The Doors and David Bowie both had a cult hit with it. Bette Midler used it for one of her character numbers on tour. You might remember it—"Show me the way to the next whisky bar / Oh, don't ask why / Oh, don't ask why / For if we don't find the next whisky bar / I tell you we must die!" A real up-with-people crowd-pleaser. Fortunately, the Brecht estate didn't really feature it as the locus of a number for Bea Arthur and a bunch of aliens, so the network didn't have to step in. Instead, Ken and Mitzie Welch, veterans of many medleys on *The Carol Burnett Show*, wrote a new song along the lines of "Those Were the Days" ("Those were the days, my friend / We thought they'd never end . . .") Sing happy, you galaxy scum.

And sing happy Bea did, right up to the last line, where she threw her arm out in a final flourish and slammed it into Cuntface, knocking him off his stool and onto the Cantina floor. Stunned, she turned and said, to no one and everyone, "I never hit a man in the cunt before."

Of course, in the retelling, she mentioned that she knew the take was never going to be used anyway, so she saw the opportunity for a joke that would never make it on the air. I think we all knew that the moment the alien did a cuntface-plant.

It seemed weird at the time, very weird, to be doing an ironic *oom-pah-pah* number about nostalgia for fellowship amongst a bunch of creatures who spent most of what turned out to be all of the *Star Wars* movies killing, maiming, lasering, and dismembering each other.

Looks like the Brecht estate had a clear view of things to come. In the context of our show, however, Bea's spot is our eleven o'clock number, the cue that things are about to wrap up.

As we return to the plot, it seems that Han and Chewie have made it to Maison Wookiee, dispatching the last remaining imperial storm-trooper—a poor imperial stuntman who breaks through a shoddily constructed banister on the Wookiee lanai and plunges to his death at the bottom of the tree, many miles below. (I did mention Lumpy walking along this very railing, which didn't look too sturdy even then.) Of course, it's clear from the shot that the guy only falls about three feet; the air mattress below is obviously not in the shot, but he doesn't seem to be in distress as he takes the dive, and in space no one can hear you scream.

Everyone is suddenly and emotionally reunited and there is a very slow and trippy sequence where all the major players are given a glowing crystal that looks like one of Diana Ross's earrings from an early Motown special. We don't know where Malla stored these, but evidently that tree house had generous and high-ceilinged closet space. The crystals are cojoined in choreography that looks something like a Mafia blood oath, and then—right after the commercial—we are transported to Wookiee Stonehenge.

The stones are a backdrop for a herd of Wookiees who emerge holding candles or crystals or crystal candles—good drag name, eh wot?—and start a religioso proceeding that turns out to be the solemn celebration of Life Day. This is not to be confused with anything festive like New Year's Eve. It's somber and meaningful. The Wookiees, and there are many of them, are clad in long red robes that completely cover their bodies, which was very convenient for the costumers who otherwise would have had to build a lot of time-consuming Wookiee fur. As it was, they just had to come up with heads, but they didn't have to be very detailed heads, because the whole thing was shot in gloomy shadow and a little out of focus. I mean, I could have stood in with my beard and curly hippie hair and passed for one of the flock, as long as I wasn't in the first row.

There is a lot of ponderous marching in circles, and at length, and I do mean length, Carrie and the boys and the droids appear, and she launches bravely into her Life Day song. And she really could sing. And act, because she manages to appear sincere about all this, which was in itself a feat. Nothing about the Princess Leia we know from the movie suggests that she would ever do anything approaching this number.

And then it was over. Across several time zones, people were shaking their heads. The smart ones were reloading their pipes. And a few people, more than a few, were feeling cheated, because they were already heavily invested in the *Star Wars* myths and this just didn't live up to any of them, nor did it really feature any of the characters they cared about or any of the special effects that had thrilled them on the big screen. It was as if *The Godfather Part II* had been made about the Irish lawyer's tender domestic life and his problems dealing with a father-in-law with gout. Though *that* guy could at least put a sentence together.

The phone didn't ring too much the weekend the show aired. It was the week before Thanksgiving, and people might have been busy slaughtering turkeys and upending pumpkins. The ones who did call were mildly amused by what they had seen. They recognized the show for what it was. The ones who really would have appreciated it were too stoned to reach for their remotes. There was no outrage. That would come years later, when the next generation of Lucasytes discovered it hidden under a pile of something on the internet.

At one point, once hardcore keyboard warfare disguised as "social media" kicked in, blogs began appearing, dragging all our names through the Kashyyykian mud, which I'm guessing they have a lot of on the Wookiee planet in order to feed all those five-hundred-foot-tall trees. Aside from the slander of copious drug use, which I myself enabled through that most powerful of tools—humor—I made it through the wormhole. But it never goes away. And it won't, as long as there are kids who grow up studying all dozen movies and the TV shows the way I grew up studying Talmud.

It will be my lightsaber to bear.

2

The Paul Lynde Halloween Special (1976)

Or, at Least We Had the Real Wicked Witch

As I said up front, if we'd known people were still going to be talking about *The Star Wars Holiday Special* forty-five years later, we, the perps, would have paid closer attention. If Paul Lynde, who moved to a galaxy far, far away in 1982, knew we were still talking about him almost a quarter of the way through the twenty-first century, he would burst his Hollywood square.

Paul never considered himself a success. He was one of the few people I've known who only seemed happy when the cameras were rolling or the curtain was up. Oh, he had moments of fun, but there was a tortured, bitter taste in his mouth that informed his comic delivery, onstage and off, and it made him a star. And he was a star. Not the star he wanted to be, but a star nonetheless. Rich, famous, and adored for being theatrically cantankerous, he was the perfect foil: the loan officer who won't come through, the landlord who tells you to fix it yourself, the curmudgeon who throws cold water on everything, the American Scrooge. He broke out on Broadway in the original 1960 production of *Bye Bye Birdie* as the exasperated father, a character who loves Ed Sullivan more than his own children. "Who wants respect from a ten-year-old kid?" he famously pleaded in his signature song, "Kids."

That he could get away with playing the father of a ten-year-old in 1960 was his real genius. Effeminate, bitchy, slightly mincy, he was more like the guncle no one talked about. Paul used this to supreme advantage when he was cast as the guncle no one talked about in a family of witches on the hit TV series *Bewitched* (1964–1972). Uncle Arthur is still an iconic figure in both gay and straight circles. On *Bewitched*, he was a supporting character. Paul was always a support-ing character on TV and in film. He became the center of attention only fleetingly, in summer stock tours of comedies originated by other actors, in revues in which he starred and introduced a bevy of sup-porting performers, and on TV specials, which is where all this is headed in a moment.

Paul was a supporting character because, really, he was a flavor. You added him as a dash of spice into whatever story you were telling. His greatest mark was made on the game show *Hollywood Squares*, where from the mid-'60s to early '80s he would come in with a one-line zinger-answer to a question. A dash of flavor. This was his unadulterated niche. It was a slightly abbreviated version of what he did in movies, but a much more lucrative one. His was not a talent designed to carry a story.

This bothered Paul, because he was an actor, but at a certain point he became Paul Lynde and could not parlay that into what he really wanted to do—*not* be Paul Lynde. This was the source of a lot of his bitterness. He had come up in New York in the '50s with guys like Mel Brooks and Woody Allen who had taken their personas and turned themselves into movie stars. Unlike Paul, they wrote their own material. He groused about them a lot. That they were Jewish didn't thrill him, either. I am Jewish, but I am also gay, so I got some sort of tarnished golden ticket. His representatives also were Jewish, and some of them were gay, so we all seemed to be in the park on the same pass.

Paul was funny and he did write, especially in his early years, mostly sketches for revues, but even if he did come up with a play or movie idea, he was who he was and expanding beyond that proved difficult. There is a theory going around that he was stymied in his efforts because he was known to be gay—nobody was publicly gay when he came up—but I don't think that applied much in Paul's case. There was only one Paul Lynde, and that model came with built-in restrictions that had more to do with style than anything else. Onstage and, in the case of *Bye Bye Birdie*, on film as well, he made for a funny caricature of a harassed parent. But it couldn't carry the picture.

It also couldn't carry a sitcom, the stars of which are usually relatable folks surrounded by crazy people. Paul tried twice in that format and struck out both times. But variety specials, those hours built around a singular talent and whatever cohorts they can muster to play with them, were perfect for him. Not weekly, just every now and again, which is why they're called specials. Paul wound up doing seven of them in four years.

The first, *The Paul Lynde Comedy Hour* (1975), was a straight-up comedy show with Jack Albertson and Nancy Walker, two other immigrants from Broadway who had become sitcom stars, and the Osmonds for some musical relief. The following year, with Paul's own ABC shows having failed, Fred Silverman—who ran all three commercial networks at one point or another—put him on the new ABC variety series he had concocted for two of the Osmonds, *Donny and Marie* (1976–1979), as comical relief. In addition, it was my understanding that the network promised him some more specials so he would not feel demoted from star to supporting player.

But the specials had to be special, something more than just sketch shows with musical interludes, something that delivered Paul's unique flavor in a controlled atmosphere. They needed a theme to give Paul material unique to that particular show. Holiday specials are all theme, none more so than the reliable stream of Christmas shows that burst out of whatever dam they're hiding behind right after Thanksgiving. But the idea of creating a celebration of peace, joy, and goodwill toward men built around a human grinch . . . just didn't ring any silver bells.

Halloween was another matter. I mean—he was already a witch! A witchy-witch was not a stretchy-stretch. A bitchy witch was even better, crafted around the parameters of what the sponsors would tolerate at 8:00 on a Friday night. Airing two days before Halloween 1976, in the time slot normally occupied by *Donny & Marie*, the special was a lead-in to the 9:00 show, a TV-movie sequel, *Look What's Happened to Rosemary's Baby*. The title alone is funnier than almost anything on TV ever.* But it was clear the heavy spookiness had to come later in the evening.

When you're doing a Paul Lynde show, it's best to open with Paul, just Paul. That's what they came for, and anything else is going to be anticlimactic. Confusion is a handy comedic device, because it leads to frustration, and frustration was Paul's long suit. Like many of us, when the Paul Lynde character, and often Paul himself, got frustrated, it almost immediately went global. He got mad at the world. And that would get him snippy. So we opened what was lavishly billed as *The Paul Lynde Halloween Special* with Paul dressed as Santa Claus trimming a Christmas tree. And singing "We Wish You a Merry

---

* *Rosemary's Baby* (1968), based on the novel of the same name, is a thriller about a coven of witches who live in the Dakota, the building on Manhattan's Upper West Side where some years later John Lennon was shot. Rosemary is the unsuspecting newlywed they find who winds up giving birth to the son of Satan. It stars Mia Farrow in an Oscar-nominated performance. It is safe to say that in 1968, it was all the rage. Eight years later, it remained current, as the TV-movie sequel was about to prove.

Christmas," in that delivery that lets you know he is wishing you nothing of the sort.

His merriment is cut short by the appearance of his housekeeper of fifteen years, played by our first guest star, Margaret Hamilton, most famous for being the original green goblin, the Wicked Witch of the West in *The Wizard of Oz* (1939). As I know you will remember, she was also Miss Gulch, the prissy schoolmarm who seized Toto right before the tornado. She looks a bit more like Gulch than the witch when she shows up as Paul's housekeeper, conveniently named Margaret. Her witchiness will be revealed after a commercial break or two.

Margaret the housekeeper is a kinder, gentler Miss Gulch, but fairly firm in her dealings with Paul. After some very long, silent takes, it is her duty to reveal to him that it is not Christmas. Confused and frustrated—remember that great comedy team?—he sends her away . . . there's always a threat that he'll boil over . . . but before he can, he thinks of another holiday that it might just be.

And here comes Peter Cottontail, not exactly hopping but moving with all deliberate speed in a huge bunny costume with a basket loaded with eggs . . . and he's foiled again by Margaret, who is pretty good at playing exasperation herself. Dismissed again, Margaret heads off just as—aha! New thought! Of course! Valentine's Day!

By now, the audience is wondering if maybe Paul will show up as a very pregnant woman going into Labor Day . . . OK, that was my pitch. I thought, if we're going to go big with this, we might as well go really big. Everybody laughed and then it was shot down, humanely and euthanasically, but permanently. And this by a roomful of genuine lunatics, but they had a practical streak.

Unlike a lot of writing staffs on comedy shows, or maybe I should say a lot of the staffs I run into today, the guys and gals (as they were still allowed to be called) who worked on these shows were often complete maniacs. A lot of them came from performing. Some of them were stealth maniacs. Steve Martin. Chevy Chase. They presented as normal people until, without warning, they would allow themselves to blossom into hilarious, crazy disruptors.

Steve and Chevy were not on staff at the Halloween show. But we had the certifiable Ronny Graham, a great cohort of Mel Brooks who had written revue material for Broadway when it still had revues, and who was known at the time of the Lynde show as Mr. Dirt, a character on commercials for Mobil Oil. In the '50s and '60s, Ronny had worked in the *New Faces* shows on Broadway with Paul. And he knew where the bodies were buried. Famously, one of them being Bing Davidson, Paul's companion who fell out of a hotel room window in San Francisco in 1965, for reasons that have been combed over for decades. Ronny had a feral grin and bounced around dispensing folderol and good cheer. He was fond of singing parody songs from his act if ever there was a pause in the conversation. So we were treated to "There's a bright golden haze on Jayne Meadows," "You'll find your life will begin the very moment you're in Ike and Tina," and "Bewitched, bothered, and Bea Arthur."

There was another Ronny, Ronny Pearlman. Not to be confused with Ron Perlman, Hellboy, the father of the Sons of Anarchy, and my costar in *The Ice Pirates*, about which more later. Neither of them is to be confused with Ronald Perelman, who later ran Revlon and was married to Claudia Cohen, a New York gossip columnist. And Ronny has been confused with the other two at least three times a day.

Ronny Pearlman was a thin guy with hair we sometimes called a Jew-fro, you know, curly and kinky and big—my tribal hair, although mine never grew out that particular way. He had back trouble and he found it easier to lie down on the office floor and write on a legal pad held just below his nose. We also enjoyed an illegal smoke now and then, and Ronny enjoyed a dalliance with Linda Ronstadt, no less, which was going on during production. Not *during* production—I mean, it was off campus, you know. Although he presented as a placid hippie, he would occasionally have bursts of surreal pitching, ideas that would bounce off the wall and rarely land in the script. But then he would throw out one crazy, wonderful line. I did a couple of other shows with him before his underlying heart problems took him in 1977.

Giving Ronny Graham—the other Ronny—a run for his insanity was Biff Manard, a tall, energetic comic/actor who also appeared in the show as an actor, under the most controlled circumstances I've ever seen him in. He looked like something off a Crosby, Stills & Nash album cover, but he was an explosive device.

Rounding out the writing team was a writing team: Sol Weinstein and Howard Albrecht. They were older than any of us and veterans of many, many sitcoms, and they looked at us like we had just got gotten off some refugee vessel from a nation that expelled anyone who ever did anything amusing. They weren't entirely sure we were part of the business as they knew it. Most of the time, they were the sedate and methodical ones, and very dry in their delivery, but occasionally Sol would, out of nowhere, become a tropical storm of craziness, with an eye twitch that was known throughout the comedy writing world. "The human traffic light," they called him.

This room that should have had padded walls was overseen by our producers, Bob Booker and George Foster. They were two guys who had worked in radio and TV and advertising in New York. Bob was Don Draper as a comedy writer. Slick, martini-drinking, Madison Avenue, always with a drop-dead one-liner. George, who was a bit older, looked like a Jewish version of Yosemite Sam who had let the mustache go silver. Soft-spoken but nuts, which I loved. They had made their fortune on maybe the biggest-selling comedy album of all time, *The First Family* (1962), which was about the Kennedys in the White House. They also did a series of comedy albums about being Jewish, which only one of them was, and later an album about being gay, which neither of them was, but I was, and I would be their partner on that particular comedy gem.

The room also included two guys who worked independent of the rest of us. Joe Byrne, a big version of Mickey Rooney, hale and hearty and full of bounce, was the producer who actually got the show produced, the one who supervised the below-the-line craftspeople, the one who knew what time lunch was. He was in on everything and was a great audience for the caged specimens in the writers' den. And there was Billy Barnes. Billy was to Los Angeles what Noël Coward was to London, a scrupulous observer of the native foibles who turned out sophisticated, epigrammatic lyrics as well as some beautiful free-standing love songs. Billy had several revues of his songs running over the years in Hollywood. But his bread and butter was the special material and parodies he wrote for TV specials.* He presented a fey, occasionally Waspish personality, but once you got to know him, he revealed himself to be a deeply sentimental soul. He had cultivated himself some armor.

But we were at Paul discovering that it's Halloween. Although we all had ideas for other holidays Paul could celebrate, Margaret finally clues him in on what time it is—a time of witches, spooks, and strange creatures of the night . . . to which Paul replies, "Sounds like *Hollywood Squares.*" And the High Halloween Day service can begin.

It starts with . . . what else? . . . a monologue. Marshall McLuhan, the media theorist who coined the phrase "the medium is the message" as well as "the global village," was heavily worshipped in the '70s, and the mighty pooh-bahs of American television took him to heart. McLuhan proposed that there were two kinds of media: hot ones and cool ones. This was before the internet and smartphones and a lot of other inventions that disrupted his theory. Television was a cool medium, because it entered your home and became part

---

* Special material: Unique songs written for TV specials or concert acts. Rarely if ever used anywhere else. One-offs.

of your surroundings and you were largely passive when watching it. The biggest stars were all pint-sized on the TV screen, and they were talking to you as if they were in the room with you. TV stars were people you wanted to hang out with. Movie stars were larger-than-life personalities projected in a different environment. We asked more of them. TV personalities were old friends having a chat with you, even if they remained in character while they did it. With few exceptions—there are always exceptions—longstanding TV stars were folks you liked having around for their positive energy.

Paul was an anomaly. He was a hot personality in a cool medium, larger than life, which is why he was most successful as a flavor in somebody else's recipe. Or as a dinner party shortstop on *Hollywood Squares*. On his own special, however, he had to engage the audience from the top. And his energy was all negative, except you knew there was going to be a joke. So far, our audience has seen him playing off his supposed housekeeper with his expected frustrations and outlandish outfits. But now he has to be the host of the party.

Dressed as if welcoming you into a suburban rec room or den (of non-iniquity), he tries to convince you that he really loves Halloween. There are a series of jokes about the holiday and his experiences with trick-or-treaters, and when we were writing this, we all realized that, aside from his surefire line readings where he hits words with his trademark elongated bleat, it's a pretty conventional welcome. We had already lit upon the idea that Paul really hated Halloween, mainly because Paul's persona hated pretty much everything. But then we decided to take a daring turn, and the idea came from Paul himself.

He told us: "When I was a kid, I was fat. Not just fat. I was *faaaaaaaaaaat*." He wanted to join in the fun, but he . . . stood out. Way out. We ran with this.

His siblings got regular costumes. His mother gave him a shower curtain. And it didn't fit. She had to let it out. And so forth. So he never felt a part of Halloween. It's just another embarrassing episode in a life of daily embarrassing episodes. It's a very real moment—and for one shining second, Paul Lynde is a cool personality, a relatable individual, not a comic device. Even, *gulp*, likeable.

Of course, as a comic device it works like gangbusters. And he comes out of it as if he really was kidding, which you knew he wasn't.

Paul really didn't *do* monologues. He wasn't a stand-up comic, but he had to welcome the home viewer, as they used to call the audience—they were still only watching TV at home back then, for the most part—so it was important that he not be alone onstage talking for too long. To remind the HV that we're in a special, we segue into a big musical number that ties in perfectly to Halloween: Paul's showstopper from *Bye Bye Birdie*, "Kids," with actual kids. Well, the "kids" of the chorus, dressed as various Halloween icons.

This was where Billy Barnes got to shine. He took the original Broadway number by Lee Adams and Charles Strouse and rewrote the lyrics to reflect what had happened to kids in the seventeen years since the song was written. And, of course, he tailored it to Paul's persona, and maybe to a little bit of his own. Let me put it this way: it ends with Paul and the dancers in a Rockettes kickline, belting out:

"There's too much Alice Cooper / Not enough Alice Faye / What's the matter with kids *to-day!*"*

And the number ends with Paul's two favorite kids, Donny and Marie Osmond, with whom he had a weekly playdate at exactly this hour of a Friday night, sneaking up on him in wizard outfits and trapping him in a garbage can like a real-life, full-sized Oscar the Grouch. Perfect casting.

After the commercial, it's time to get really Halloweenie. And for there to be an actual plot. Well, a quasi-plot, something to hang a lot of Halloween on. Margaret, dressed so she could step into a Miss

---

* Alice Faye was the first big movie musical star on the 20th Century-Fox lot. She was all-American sweetheart beautiful. Off-screen, she was sharp and funny and much married.

Marple mystery at any moment, drives Paul up to her sister's place to get him away from all those pesky kids he was pretending to love. It's far out in the country. (Paul: "We must be way out of town by now. You're hitting fewer people.") It's a house that screams Halloween, an old pile called Gloomsbury Manor. The set is astonishing. I look at it today and realize it must have cost a fortune to build and dress, especially considering what would happen to it in the course of the show. Most of the specials done back then were over-the-top spectacles, but this one . . .

Margaret's sister turns out to be, and you may be ahead of us, Witchiepoo. This is not a euphemism for irritable bowel syndrome. This is a character dreamt up by the Krofft Brothers, Sid and Marty, who will figure large in the next chapter of this confessional. Marty was the practical one who had to execute the wild ideas that came out of Sid, the stoned one. Sid is one of the world's great puppeteers and made his bones on Broadway as a solo act—in an ice show!—before he teamed with his brother to do something unheard of: adult puppet shows. Yes, before *Avenue Q* there was *Les Poupées de Paris* . . . topless showgirl puppets. They presaged breast implants. None of the boobs moved. They were quite a thing as they toured the country in the early '60s, and they brought the boys to Hollywood and into variety television, where Sid's bizarre creations could flower in shows like *H.R. Pufnstuf* (1969–1970) and *Lidsville* (1971–1973).

Witchiepoo was one of the landmark Krofft inventions. She was a good witch, not threatening, but she was very much the mistress of her domain. She bore a striking resemblance to Mammy Yokum, a character out of Al Capp's long-running cartoon strip *Li'l Abner* (1934–1977), which was hugely popular in its day but is remembered now mostly by people who performed in their high school production of the Broadway musical version. Short and feisty, Mammy ruled, just like Wilhelmina W. Witchiepoo. Coincidentally, Witchiepoo was played by Billie Hayes, who had played Mammy in the popular 1959 movie version of the Broadway musical adaptation of *Li'l Abner*.*

Strange that Margaret the housekeeper would have a sister who was Witchiepoo? Who else would be living in Gloomsbury Manor? My vote went to Mrs. Danvers, the housekeeper from Hitchcock's *Rebecca*, but I think she dies in the end, and in any event, Judith Anderson was unavailable. I think she was doing a soap opera.

The other reason it's not strange is that, at this moment, with a magic special effect, Margaret Hamilton is revealed to be the Wicked Witch of the West—which everyone knows, except apparently not Paul. "You're *wit-ches!*" he exclaims, looking back and forth at both of them. There is something insanely delightful about him not catching on sooner, especially since Margaret has been changing his linen for fifteen years, but some women really know how to keep a secret.

Now, you may be thinking it's all incredibly convenient that Margaret has brought him into the bosom(s) of family, but there is more at work here. Like all witches, they need something from him. They've seen him as Uncle Arthur on *Bewitched* and have realized that he is the perfect vessel to pour forth their message that witches have been wronged all these years and are, in fact, the victims of bad PR. He's not buying it, at first, and recites a litany of the bad things they've done, especially what Margaret did to Dorothy and, in one of my favorite line readings ever, her little dog "*To-to.*" "She asked for it" is Margaret's indignant reply.

Soon we are introduced to Gloomsbury Manor's majordomo, Billy Barty. Billy the butler comes in bearing a silver tray with some witches' brew with clouds billowing above the rim. Paul declines the

---

* If you've ever heard of Sadie Hawkins Day, you've heard of *Li'l Abner*. The comic strip was set in the hillbilly paradise of Dogpatch, USA, and the big annual event in those parts was named after the ugliest girl in town, who could never find a man. Once a year, all the single women of Dogpatch were allowed to hunt down their man of choice, who if caught, had to marry them. An efficient way of increasing the population.

drink ("I don't smoke"), and there begins an adversarial relationship between the two.

If you don't know already, now is the time to reveal that Billy Barty was a three-foot-eleven individual and probably the most famous little person in show business. He was a pint-sized combination of Edgar G. Robinson as Little Caesar and W. C. Fields as anything. Before Hervé Villechaize and Mini-Me, there was Billy paving the way. It would be hard to know if a guy like Billy could have any sort of major show business career today, although Wee Man is about the closest possibility.* Billy was a vaudeville comedian, but all the jokes and situations were built around his size. And nobody has tried this lately, because it doesn't fit neatly into a woke world. Sid and Marty adored Billy and used him in as many of their shows as they could. He was a hoot to be around, a tireless practical joker, and a physical comic who knew how to punctuate every line with some little something that made it better than it was. And I didn't mean to use *little* in any punny way.

He was also a professional letch, or played that role, reveling in the reputation he had created for himself, whether it was real or imagined. Billy was Mormon and married to the same Mrs. Barty for many years and had two kids, but he got a lot of mileage out of pretending to chase whatever skirt he could reach. We would talk about famous bombshells of Hollywood and he would muse, "Yeah, I went up on her."

My favorite story was one he attributed to my great friend Julie Newmar, who in 1966 made an indelible mark as the very first, one-and-only, original Catwoman on the iconic *Batman* TV series. She also drew eyeballs as the world's most statuesque robot on a sitcom called *My Living Doll* (1964–1965), as well as on Broadway and in big-screen

---

* Jason "Wee Man" Acuña was Johnny Knoxville's sidekick in the *Jackass* movies, but he spent most of his time being a human cannonball or pincushion and always in pain.

outings in the aforementioned *Li'l Abner* musical as Stupefyin' Jones, a citizen of Dogpatch who is so stunning, men look at her and promptly turn to stone. The revenge of Lot's wife. Without the salt.

Oh, yeah, the story. One day on a project they both worked on (I frankly don't remember which one), during a quiet moment between shots, Billy told Julie that he wanted to, yes, go up on her. And Julie looked down at him and said, "If you do, and I find out about it . . ."

Very little work was done that day.

On our show, as soon as Billy exits, after kicking Paul in the shins, because that's what Billy Barty did a lot of, the plot grinds into motion with the appearance of a performer almost as ribald—but in a sly, tasteful way—as Billy: Betty White.

When I tell most people Betty White was as sexually charged a personality as you've ever seen, they tend to be shocked, as most people think of her as Rose on *The Golden Girls*, where the sexually charged one was Rue McClanahan and Betty was the dumb one. But if you followed her career before and after that landmark show, you wouldn't be surprised at all. She was never more than a foul pitch away from a double entendre or a remark that stretched passive-aggressive to the borders of its territory. As a kid, I watched her on *Life with Elizabeth* (1953–1955), where she was a dainty and slightly scatterbrained all-American Eisenhower-era housewife. But then in 1973 her turn on *The Mary Tyler Moore Show*, as a Martha Stewart–like happy homemaker who was really a pit viper when aroused, changed all that.

Betty was a big fan of Paul's, maybe because their personae at the time were both rooted in anger. Paul's was couched in haplessness, but Betty's came from the knowledge that the only way to get what she wanted was to be in control of every situation and that you attract bears with honey, even if it's artificially flavored. We wanted Betty on the show because, well, she was Betty White, but also because we knew the two styles could play well off each other.

But we only had her for a day, so we had to contrive one scene, one costume, and something that didn't require a whole of lot of production—props, effects, rehearsal, you know. And that led us to making her Miss Halloween 1976, an actual good witch, in white. She bears a striking resemblance to Billie Burke (not to be confused with Billy Barty, or Billie Hayes or Billy Barnes, if you're just picking up the book after a nap) as Glinda in *The Wizard of Oz*. We couldn't afford to put her in a bubble and float her across the room—truthfully, we could, but how much of a rip-off would MGM tolerate?—so we had her enter in a slightly nausea-inducing whirling white blob with her head in the middle until it landed and revealed her in all her good witchiness.

It seems she was summoned by the weird sisters to meet Paul Newman. Or so she thinks. She probably wouldn't have come for this particular Paul. She's taken all the trouble to swirl in, and after a bit of sparring with our star, she's just as happy to swirl out again. And that was Betty White's appearance—literally an appearance, followed swiftly by a disappearance. They do this sort of thing on *SNL* all the time, and for the same reason: to capitalize on the current heat of any one personality.

But then comes the plot! The remaining weird sisters set about making this particular Paul the PR spokesman for Gloomsbury Manor. It's part of an effort to clear up the horrible reputation witches have carried for, oh, centuries. To sweeten the cauldron, they offer Paul three wishes—he's already had three witches . . . sorry—three carrots in front of the donkey, to get him to say yes.

Here's the dumb genius of it: whatever he wishes will set up three set pieces on the show—wasn't that clever of us? I would love to say we were the first ones to use this particular device, but I can't, and the bad news is we weren't the last ones to use it. In television, that counts for a lot.

In addition to giving us three reasons to have act breaks for commercials, this little ploy gave us at least three different scenarios to fill up with guest stars, always good on a variety show, and especially good on one starring Paul, who, I may have opined earlier, was a flavor, and an overpowering one, a little of which goes a long way.

With the exception of the brief sight-gag costumes at the top of the show, Paul has more or less been Paul, dressed in that preppy style of the '70s that men over forty were featuring. Knowing we could take that just so far, we decided to give him some characters to play that would put him in ridiculous outfits, hairstyles, and situations. This would give him laughs that didn't come from the fake-nasty zingers that were his specialty. It was one way to take care of that flavor problem.

The first is the most ridiculous. We made him a trucker. If you think that was a long haul for the audience to make, you're not just being punny. It was on our minds that the thing the audience was least expecting, and the thing that would really make them laugh, was to cast Paul in a role that was the polar opposite of their image of him. A coarse, butch—OK, sort of butch—redneck behind the wheel of a powerful machine was not how you pictured Paul Lynde. So that's the picture we put him in.

At this point in American life, the trucker was enjoying unprecedented popularity. Truck culture was everywhere. A song called "Convoy" was number one on the hit parade. Truckers were viewed as urban cowboys and pseudo-outlaws, especially when they began installing citizens band radios in their cabs and passed the time chatting with each other in their own secret code as they elbowed everybody else off the road. "Breaker breaker!" and "10-4!" became iconic mating calls between these self-styled marauders of the open highway. What more perfect thing to do with Paul Lynde than make him a trucker? But not just any old trucker. The Rhinestone Trucker. This was a play on the glittery new country singers who were known as rhinestone cowboys. It just got more and more Paul.

Paul's version of a trucker owes a lot to Elton John, and probably a bit to Wolfman Jack, the deejay who also hosted a late-night weekend

TV show. We put him in a very red wig and astonishing eyebrows and a white suit festooned with rhinestones and, well, he was a vision. Big Red, we called him. He made no sense at all, but that was the fun. Flamboyant and suitable bash bait at every truck stop, he somehow has made a name for himself as one mean mother trucker. He is racing to his favorite pit stop to marry his favorite waitress at midnight, but he has to get there before his rival, who also seems to think he is marrying her at midnight. The rival is Tim Conway.*

Of course you want to know who this girl *is* whose two top choices for husband are Paul Lynde and Tim Conway. I'd love to say it's Florence Henderson, but she comes later. It's the flame-haired Roz Kelly, who was better known, and always will be better known, as Fonzie's girlfriend on *Happy Days*: Pinky Tuscadero. Since she was so well known as Pinky Tuscadero, we decided to cast her as Pinky, truck stop siren, a very close relative of Pinky Tuscadero. That was in case anybody asked. Nobody would, because we were on ABC and so was *Happy Days* and these things run in the family.

Roz was very funny and could really sing and could really dance, as she demonstrated a couple of times in our show. She also had a great throwaway attitude and a way of firing out a put-down that had been perfected by Cher, who still uses it today. It is based in truth, as only a girl from New York named Kelly playing a girl from Milwaukee named Tuscadero could tell you.

The race to win her hand ends with what was a spectacular effect for a TV special: Paul crashing his truck through a wall of the set, braking just short of the pie holders and waving jauntily from the cab to announce his arrival. It was an actual truck, by the way, and it took up most of the soundstage, which is why the diner looks a little

---

* The very meek and very funny Tim Conway was a staple of *The Carol Burnett Show*. He specialized in extreme portraits of unfathomably dumb and inarticulate people. This gave him a lot of room for very specific physical comedy built around the idiosyncrasies he managed to find in each character. Pretty genius.

cramped on camera. Dancers doubling as diners jumped out of the way as Paul barreled through, but they didn't have very far to leap.

There follows a lot of Paul and Tim and Roz insulting each other, with Tim getting the short end of it, as his character is pretty stupid—he loved playing those. You must be chafing to know with whom Roz winds up. Paul, of course. Not only is he dripping with rhinestones—she *is* a truck stop waitress—but he has a contract to play himself in the movies and there'll be more baubles coming her way. But before she decides, there is a heart-stopping moment in which the owner and short-order cook, that short order himself, Billy Barty, emerges to single-handedly push the truck back outside. Strength always appeals to the fair sex, evidently. But fame and fortune appeal more. Paul will even find a role in the movie for his rival—the pal who doesn't get the gal. The movie, by the way, is titled *Deep Truck*.*

So Paul's wish is fulfilled and the sketch is over, but . . . to make sure the audience *knows* it's over, we added a musical number—what else but an ol' fashioned hoedown. Why, you might ask, with a scratch of the head? Where does it say "hoedown" in Halloween? It's because back before today's narrowcasting, where a show only has to appeal to its niche, you had to have something for everybody. And if you're going to do a sketch about red state people, you needed a red meat musical number to close it, because it was something that audience could embrace, even if they had been mildly offended by the stereotypes. That was how you kept sponsors happy in the broadcasting era. And sponsors were everything. They still matter just as much today on network TV, or linear TV, as it is now called when it's not

---

* *Deep Truck*—a not-so-inside reference to *Deep Throat* (1972), the most controversial film of the period, starring Linda Lovelace, about whom movies have since been made. It was a porn, but it wound up being the center of significant censorship cases that helped change the laws governing pornography. Many celebrities rallied around this freedom of speech issue, but my favorite reaction was from Pauline Kael, the *New Yorker* film critic who told me she shed a tear for "the people whose movies will not pass the standards set by this case and will therefore go to jail for not having talent."

being called legacy TV by snarky millennials who watch it anyway, but the strategy is different in the new world of a thousand niche alternatives to the networks. Today, let's say you make tampons. I know, it's a fantasy career, but indulge yourself for a moment. You, tampon-maker, want to buy commercial time on a show like *Riverdale*, where virtually every viewer is a newly eligible tampon buyer, except for the gay men who tune in for the two or three scenes of shirtless twentysomething "teens" that appear in every episode. They are not your customers, but they may know someone who is. Everybody else is a slam-dunk potential patron. Back in the day, we were making commercial television for every segment of the unwashed masses, which is also why there might have been so many commercials for detergents. Aspirational, you know.

When we come back from the hoedown, the weird sisters are deep into literature—one of them is reading *Rosemary's Baby* (a subtle plug for the show that will follow) and the other *The Exorcist*. And they are having a rollicking good time. For them, both books are inside jokes.

Paul magically appears and they quiz him about his adventures like you might ask your parents how they liked their cruise. They listen patiently and ask him if he wouldn't like to hear a little chamber music. "Where are the musicians?" he asks. "Locked up in a little chamber," they reply. We are now in total Halloween mode. And the musicians descend in an actual elevator, in an homage to Tim Curry's unforgettable entrance in *The Rocky Horror Picture Show* (1975). Or a steal, but why would anyone steal something so obvious? It has to be an homage. So we have driven a truck through a wall and built a working elevator and dressed it as a torture chamber, so it's clear there have been some bucks spent on this show. And the bucks don't stop there, for in the elevator is . . . KISS.*

---

* KISS was the hottest thing in pop rock at the time. They wore black leather, monsterish makeup, and black boots with seven-inch heels and maybe even spurs. They were loud, but they were fun and over the top and knew it. It was all

This was the band's first network television appearance. In the days before MTV and the worldwideinternetweb and enjoying *Avatar* on your Apple Watch, this was a big deal. You had to seek out the rare opportunities to view certain performers. There weren't seven nightly talk shows and a bunch of morning and afternoon arenas that showcased people. And you were just beginning to be able to tape things and watch them at your leisure. All television was appointment television. And quite a few fans made an appointment to watch KISS.

Paul had never heard of them. But he understood that if you were gonna attract a younger audience, you had to have something younger than an old witch to show them. He did have the proper level of curiosity about them, and when he had been shown pictures of their makeup, he was intrigued. He wasn't around when they rehearsed, but he did emerge when they came down to run through the number in full costume and makeup before we let the audience in.

I sat with him in the unoccupied bleachers to drink it all in. The first chords from the band were deafening and Paul winced, but it was almost a stage wince, something he did in character now and again. There was a lot of smoke and exploding lights and he watched with increased fascination for about half a minute and, just before he could lose interest, Gene Simmons, the lead singer, came way downstage and stuck out his tongue right at Paul. Gene Simmons's tongue, then and now, should have its own Wikipedia page. It is a red carpet to hell. Very long, very agile, very serpent in the Garden of Eden. A tongue for the ages. Paul was transfixed. He grabbed my arm and said, in a classic line reading, "I would like to *meeeeet* him." It was classic because, like so many of Paul's lines, it said nothing but also said everything.

---

theater. The president of their fan club came in for the network television debut and we were all a bit deflated to find that he was the son of Ringo Starr. Deflated because it made us all feel as ancient as the witches.

When the smoke and the commercials clear, we're back at Gloomsbury Manor, where the unholy three, having recovered from Gene Simmons's mother tongue, are embroiled in a game of Monopoly. After Paul lands on Dark Place, Margaret announces this game is boring and she's going out to see her favorite horror movie, *The Sound of Music*. Paul gets fed up—I know you were counting the seconds until that happened—and says he wishes he were anywhere else, like in the middle of the desert. Uh-oh. That's wish #2. As a favor, the witches also grant wish #2a, that he is—prepare yourself—a rich, romantic sheik like in the (old, silent) movies. If we were doing it today, he'd become Mohammed bin Salman, without the romantic part.

You may be asking was this really Paul's wish, or was it the best he could come up with when he realized he was trapped. Moot point, students. It was a way to get him into another ridiculous costume, wig, and role. What's Halloween without costumes, wigs, and roles?

To make things even more ridiculous, this self-described chic sheik is pursuing his elegant veddy veddy upper class English rose: who else but Florence Henderson?

Yes, Carol Brady, America's wholesome mother of six, nailed the part. I'm pretty sure none of you absorbing this have ever thought of Florence as a glamorous high-society Londoner turned siren of the desert sands, but Florence never thought of herself as Carol Brady, and that was why she was willing to do sketches like this—to demonstrate to an audience that had discovered her on *The Brady Bunch* (1969–1974) that she was way more than that sitcom character.

From the moment she was auditioned by Rodgers and Hammerstein, who cast her in a touring production of *Oklahoma!* in 1952, Florence had been a musical comedy star. A gorgeous soprano, she was an American Julie Andrews—actually, there is a case for saying Julie Andrews was a British Florence Henderson, as they both came up on Broadway almost simultaneously. In fact, Hollywood tried to make Florence the literal American Julie Andrews when they put her in a huge movie musical taken from a Broadway hit, *Song of Norway* (1970), in which she, too, got to run through the mountains in a dirndl while belting her lungs out. Didn't quite work.

Like Dame Julie, the dame that was Florence had a bawdy side, and they both kept it hidden from their audiences but not from their friends and coworkers. Florence had four children from her marriage to Ira Bernstein, who handled the business side of the Shubert theatrical organization, so she had seen a great deal inside show biz and was a much more colorful mother than Carol Brady. But she knew what her image was, so she kept at her side a small repertoire of dirty jokes with which she liked to surprise the unsuspecting. OK, risqué jokes. Hearing her tell them made them seem dirtier than they were.

She was, of course, gorgeous, and in this particular sketch, I couldn't keep from stealing a line from Noël Coward, who when he met Peter O'Toole said, "My dear, you are so pretty, they should call the picture *Florence of Arabia*." Naturally, we had Paul use that name to describe himself, and he wasn't far off, looking like a young Vincent Price playing Valentino.*

The real Florence is a revelation, for those of you who only know her as Carol Brady. She is actually acting in this piece, playing high style with an accent. She maintains a straight face, even when she announces she is Lady Westinghouse, heir to a great fortune, to which Paul replies that she is so icy she's the Westinghouse Frigidairess.

An elaborate seduction follows, which is where Paul surprised us all by doing some acting, too. He begins describing all the wonderful things he's going to do to Florence and suddenly discovers that

---

* That's Rudolph Valentino, the great silent screen lover, not Valentino Garavani, the dress designer and owner of multiple pugs (there's a documentary that tells all). Valentino was the first truly legendary film star. His name became synonymous with romance and seduction. He may also have been the first Hollywood star to die tragically young, setting a template that continues to this day. While we're here, I should note that Meryl Streep told the *Florence of Arabia* story at the Oscars when she presented a special award to Peter O'Toole. What goes around . . .

. . . he's turning himself on. It's a neat piece of character work and a reminder that there was more to him than his trademark schtick. And it ends in a kiss.

Back then, when casting directors and production executives were looking for leading men and there was some unspoken question about the actor's sexual persuasion, someone would say, "Can he kiss the girl?" This was code for *I hear he's light in the loafers, will the audience buy him in a love scene?* It is no doubt still used today. To be fair, it is also used to describe any man who is not a traditional leading man type—and, to be cruelly fair, its reverse is used to describe any woman who may not be a conventional object of desire. Before you take up cudgels, remember that movies are a commercial enterprise, and the last thing anyone wants to do is turn off the audience. Therefore, the last thing anyone does is to actually trust the audience to be able to separate fantasy from reality. Bambi's mother isn't really dead.*

So, Paul tells the girl he's going to kiss her . . . and he does . . . for quite a long moment. And nobody titters, until Florence comes out of the kiss and, like nothing has happened, says, "I'm ready whenever you are."

Before the seduction can get any steamier, the hot couple is interrupted by, yes, Tim Conway, as Seymour of the French Foreign Legion. His French is evidently quite foreign, as he speaks with a heavy Quebec accent. Once again, Paul has met his nemesis and it is Tim. He is dragged off on some petty charge, but returns a moment later (after a moment of heavy emoting by Florence). Why did suddenly Seymour release him? Paul gave him his pet cockatoo.

"A man gets mighty lonely in the Foreign Legion," Paul says to us with almost a wink . . . right before he sweeps Florence into his arms.

---

* Today, there is a minor kerfuffle in the bubble-dwelling activist community of keyboard warriors about gay actors playing straight parts, straight actors playing gay parts, nonbinary act— You get the picture. There were no publicly out gay actors in 1976. It's always dangerous to conflate politics with art. In most cases, it's anti-art.

And scene. And Paul has gotten his second wish.

What happens after the next commercial is so surreal and so roller coaster that it almost passeth description. It is really the sort of thing that could only happen on a mid-'70s variety special. It starts traditionally enough, with Margaret telling Billy Barty to put the house to bed for the night, starting with the lions, tigers, and bears, oh my, that serve as pets—they make a racket, but it turns out not to be the menagerie at all, but merely Margaret's mother, unseen, but very much heard. After all that Paul returns from the desert, and this is where the unthinkable begins. Paul turns nice.

He's even sweet, playing a note that I can't recall him playing ever before. He decides that for his third wish, he would like to give the witches their wish. They are, of course, dumbfounded. No one's ever wanted to do anything for them before.

I don't remember whose idea it was to give Paul at least a moment of out-of-character realness, but I do remember Paul going for it in a big way. His reaction to the pitch was almost the same as the witches: he'd never done anything nice for anybody before, at least not onstage or on camera. It was a wholly novel idea. He couldn't resist.

The witches are flattered, but they don't know he can accomplish this. Simple. He grabs what Witchiepoo is holding and says, "Where there's a wand, there's a way." And poof. We are in their wish. Surreal moment #2.

Surreal moment #3 comes when we see the results of that wish. They want to go to a Hollywood disco, but they never get out of the house. Old Gloomsbury Manor is magically transformed into—a disco!, replete with orange neon bats. They descend on the elevator—you didn't think we were going to spend all that money on only one entrance, did you?—in witchy black tie and enter into a sea of dancers in elegant Halloween disco wear. There will be lots of shaking of everyone's groove thing, but first a special guest entertainer is going to perform, and that is, yes, Florence Henderson, this time in

jet-black beading to sing—brace yourself—"That Old Black Magic."
Not a tune anyone ever would associate with Flo.

OK, let's review. By this point in the hour, the audience has
bought the traditional tropes that there are good witches and that
they grant wishes. They have also, hopefully, embraced the notion
that witches can be funny, can have human feelings and needs, and
can afford the mortgage on a mountaintop estate. That witches like
disco, that Florence Henderson can swing jazz, that Paul Lynde is
a nice guy who helps old ladies—these are the buys they are asked
to make.

If you had sampled any of the mind-altering substances, from
bourbon to bongs, that many of us back then had, then all of this
would make perfect sense to you. What amazes me is that, for nearly
five decades, people who have done none of those things accept all of
this as a perfectly plausible scenario. Disbelief has evidently gone off
and rented an Airbnb somewhere. It's not just suspended, it's canceled.

And to prove that, once Flo has finished casting her spell, KISS
returns . . . to do a ballad! Yes, they had one big ballad hit, a solo
called "Beth," sung by Peter Criss to his own piano accompaniment.
It's a sad song, a lament from a musician on the road to the girl waiting for him at home (unless somewhere there is a guy named Beth),
all about how miserable this musician is accepting the adoration of
thousands. Peter sang and played it in full KISS makeup and leather
drag, at the keyboard, suitably dimmed disco lighting all around him.
It made absolutely no sense at all, so it fit right in. We all thought it
was a bit odd for KISS to do this particular song, but it was a monster
hit, their biggest single ever, and it was #7 on the Billboard charts
when the show aired, so go fight that. The fact that it had nothing
whatever to do with our show was irrevocably irrelevant. I mean, it
followed Florence Henderson.

Their next song, a screamer called "King of the Nighttime World,"
was much more in keeping. Yes, there was room for three KISS songs

in this variety special. That's how popular KISS was to a segment of the audience that ABC desperately wanted to attract. *Get 'em young* is always the mantra of Madison Avenue. Start introducing them to your product when they're kids and they may stay with you for a lifetime, especially if it's a product they won't outgrow.

Once, when working on a different show that was produced by Sid and Marty Krofft, the head writer gave all the other writers as a Christmas present a little framed wall hanging. It was a piece of paper under glass, and on the paper was a feather, a balloon, and a handful of sprinkle glitter confetti. There was a small toy hatchet hanging from one side of the frame. On the glass was a small printed message: Break in Case of Finale.

Every variety show had a finale, a big moment when all the guests assembled in whatever costumes they had worn earlier and sang something and hugged each other and maybe tugged their ear, or gave the audience some sort of signature goodbye. These actions were almost always accompanied by blowing feathers, falling balloons, or snowing glitter confetti. You wouldn't think of ending a show without them. It would be like a seder without matzo.*

The Halloween special ended with all these things, and to go with them, the semi-obligatory 1976 disco finale. You might have seen this coming when the witches asked to go to a Hollywood disco. This wish did not come out of thin or thick air.† "Disco Lady" was a big hit then, and it had a sort of laid-back beat, one that all our principals could move to without too much trouble. Unfortunately, it also had a troubling lyric: "Shake it up, shake it down / Move it in, move it round, disco lady."

---

* Sidebar joke Ray Charles used to tell: "They gave me a piece of matzo once. I said, 'Who wrote this shit?'"
† Smog levels in Los Angeles were at their highest in the 1970s, before the catalytic converter was introduced.

The network censors, often on the writers' side, suggested maybe changing it to "disco baby" so it wasn't about anything a lady was doing, or shouldn't be doing. We took their advice, and the witches and their newfound friends are able to boogie without a care in the underworld that they are offending anybody.

Paul winds up the show by thanking all of his guests, and then, in a little speech that bookends his childhood story ("*faaaaaaaaaaat*"), thanks the audience at home for making him feel wanted, implying that he hasn't felt wanted since childhood. I thought it a little over the top, but he did have a couple of sincere moments in the show, and I know Paul did want to be wanted. I thought of giving him Jackie Vernon's joke: Jackie was a deadpan comic who told jokes in a monotone, never breaking character, mostly about himself. One of my favorites was "When I was a kid, I was unwanted. Now I'm wanted in thirteen states." But I wasn't about to lift Jackie's joke, and it seemed a little late in the day for Paul to be making another joke about being an unhappy kid, so the little over-the-top moment remained . . . and Paul played it beautifully.

Paul did five more specials after this one, but the Halloween show has a resonance that stuns everyone who was involved with it. It is not part of some iconic canon like *The Star Wars Holiday Special*. Paul has been dead for four decades. Since I more or less inherited his spot as the gay square on the Whoopi Goldberg iteration of *Hollywood Squares* at the turn of the millennium, Paul's name comes up in my conversations more than it does in yours. Most people who were around remember him vividly, but only when someone mentions his name, and most people rarely do.

The internet has kept him alive, usually in the form of an email that shows up periodically with a list of the great "ad-libs" Paul made on *Squares*. These are fun, but there's usually a subject line like "Who needs writers?" or "When that show was really funny" or "What a mind!" Let them believe what they want to believe.

What's interesting is the volume of people I have heard from who were born years after Paul died who have discovered him on the internet. For so many of them, their first encounter with Paul is the Halloween special. They then go and find all the other stuff. Having worked with Bette Midler since the Paleozoic Era, I can tell you that a similar thing happened to her with the witchy family comedy *Hocus Pocus* (1993). A quick disappointment thirty years ago, released for some crackpot reason in the middle of the summer, it then enjoyed repeated showings on cable TV and later the internet and acquired a positive reputation from a generation whose parents saw it as kids and for whom it has become a viewing tradition. And a billion-minutes-viewed streaming sequel in 2022. Go know.

Obviously, the winner here is Halloween, which has, thanks to television, become a national holiday in which everybody gets to put on drag—Republicans, too—and have a good ol' time that doesn't need to involve a whole lot of mind-altering substances the way Mardi Gras or New Year's Eve does. We unwittingly all have stumbled into a tradition that gay people secretly called the Bitches Christmas. The Halloween special was more a celebration of that than anything else.

3

The Brady Bunch Hour
(1976-1977)

Or, at Least We Didn't Have Cousin Oliver

The Manhattan Transfer transferred me to Los Angeles. If you're wondering what that means, let me explain. The Transfer are a musical quartet that started out fifty years ago doing what was loosely called "nostalgia," which in this context means songs from previous decades, which they did faithfully but with such brilliant vocal and instrumental arrangements that everything seemed brand new.

It helped that each of them was a knockout singer. There were two girls and two boys and they dressed up in formal wear of the 1930s, like they just stepped out of one of those gigantic nightclub sets in a Depression-era musical. There was a bald jive master, a suave crooner, a willowy redhead, and a tiny firecracker, and their stage act was lit, which didn't mean then what it means now, but you know what I mean. Fred Silverman, later to greenlight *The Paul Lynde Halloween Special*, was running CBS at the time—remember, he captained all three commercial networks at one time or another, and I bumped into him at all three. Fred strongly believed in the notion of *teams hosting variety shows*, and he thought the Transfer would make a terrific one of those. So he bought four shows to run over the month of August 1975, in the Sunday-night time slot then occupied by Cher. She was going it alone—as was Sonny, on another network and, um, opposite her. Cher was winning. History has made that abundantly clear.

Summer was always a good time to cheaply try out new shows that, if they caught on, could be plugged into the fall schedule the minute one of the programs already in the pipeline was injured in the ratings. Benchwarmers, they were. So I came out to L.A. to sit on the bench with the Transfer and put together a show. We discovered when the first one aired that the world was not ready to buy these four kids dressed up like they were doing a sketch about Fred Astaire and Ginger Rogers, especially when the world could be watching *The Six Million Dollar Man* or *The Wonderful World of Disney* at 7:30 on a hot summer Sunday night when the sun was still out. But the town loved it.

When people in Hollywood talk about "the town," they mean the show business bubble in which nearly everyone on the west side of Los Angeles dwells. Everywhere I went, people were talking about how hip the show was, how great the music was, how *swinging* the music was. *The Carol Burnett Show* even did a parody of the show in its fall premiere, with Burnett, Harvey Korman, Tim Conway, and Vicki Lawrence in high duds singing "Tuxedo Junction," the Transfer's signature tune. But the odds never were in our favor.

Ultimately it didn't matter. After the show disappeared, the Transfer recorded a cover of a smooth '50s pop hit called "Chanson D'Amour," which became a global sensation and had them filling up bullrings in Barcelona. This led them to an unprecedented career creating albums in every musical style, from vocalese to Brazilian to emo to symphonic. They eventually carved their own, multi-Grammy-winning niche as a jazz act—which they kept doing for fifty years, until their group retirement in 2024.

But when they attempted variety television in the '70s, the public didn't really buy it. The town did, on a personal level, but the town didn't know what to do with them, and the town got a little scared when the general public didn't warm up to the ManTran. Too hip. That was the whisper. I mean, "we" loved it, but it's too hip for the average audience. Anybody who was involved with the show was also deemed too hip and not a safe bet to deliver the kind of shows that sponsors liked.

I found this out during a week of meetings on a variety of variety shows—there were a bunch of them on the air then—when I was repeatedly told how hip I was and how too hip I was to write a show for, just to mention one, the Captain & Tennille. Another one of Fred Silverman's team-host gets, Toni Tennille and Daryl "the Captain" Dragon had a string of pop hits—you can't deny remembering Muskrat Susie and Muskrat Sam, can you?—and they turned them into a weekly variety show. I went back to my West Hollywood apartment with the thin walls and the open windows and the friendly neighborhood hairdressers banging each other and shrieking in notes Callas would have killed to reach. I was too hip.

About a year later, I volunteered this information one night at dinner with Florence Henderson. Well, not all of what I just told you, but the "too hip" part. She nodded with great wisdom and said, "I know how you feel." Now, I never thought Florence, talented as she was, was anyone who would be labeled "too hip." In private, absolutely, but her performing persona was all-American, sunny, and blemish free. I think she may have been yanking my chain, as the hipper kids used to say. I got firmer in my conviction when she said, "Come and write The Brady Bunch. No one will ever say you're too hip again."

She had to be joking, and not just about the idea of someone like me writing The Brady Bunch. The show had been canceled in 1974, and it had not yet become something you could reliably expect to see in reruns at least once a day on some channel or other. It was a series that had ripened on its own vine and was now withering away at some retirement vineyard in Florida. More fool I. Florence revealed that the show was getting a variety show reboot courtesy of, here he comes again, Fred Silverman.

Actually, I believe he *wanted* to reboot *The Partridge Family*. That was the show that *followed* the Bradys on Friday nights in the '70s. It was also about a family with a blonde matriarch—Shirley Jones—but they were a performing family. David Cassidy, Shirley's son on the show and stepson in real life, broke out of the show as a major teeny-bop heartthrob. Neither he nor his stepmom wanted to be part of a variety series in which they continued playing Partridges. No matter how many times the ABC bankers said, "C'mon, get happy"—the show's earworm theme song—they resisted. So Fred turned to the other family in the Friday family hour, the Bradys.

To be fair, the Bradys were not without their bona fides. The six kids who made up the blended family had toured in a concert act that played state fairs and other one-offs, but they were not the Osmonds or the Jacksons or even Fink's Mules, an act George Burns had toured with in vaudeville of which he was particularly fond. It's probably rude to put the Bradys in the same category as an animal act, but at least I'm not comparing them to the Aristocrats.

They could sing and dance, some of them quite well—Greg (Barry Williams) and Marcia (Maureen McCormick)—and others enough to get by in the bosom of family. But this six-pack of kids was not enough to carry a weekly variety show. The real talent, of course, was Mom, Florence, a triple threat. And then there was Dad.

The Partridge Family didn't have a dad. The Brady dad was a skilled comedic and dramatic actor, Robert Reed, whose career was not going where he wanted it to go when he signed on to the original series. It was nothing he ever envisaged, he told me himself, but during the show's initial run, he became foster dad to these six kids, running interference with their actual parents as well as producers. He loved the idea of working with them again. He had not the slightest interest in singing or dancing, both of which of course he would cruelly be forced to do every week, meaning he looked forward to Monday table reads of the script with all the joy of a prisoner about to be waterboarded. But he was game.

Florence, who was raising four kids and eager to be at home as much as possible, had taken the original series for just that reason, and she jumped into the variety show with enthusiasm. This time she got to sing and dance as well as wrestle a pot roast. What neither of them actually knew when they were offered the show was . . . what was the show going to be?

The original show was about how you blended two families with three kids apiece into one household indivisible with liberty and justice for all, plus a lot of sports, dating, getting into jams, defying parental authority, reasserting parental authority, playing tricks on the maid, playing tricks on the other siblings in cahoots with the maid, blowing things up, embarrassing Dad, infuriating Mom, and notice nowhere in there is mentioned singing, dancing, or hosting a variety show. Just nowhere.

Yet that was the task at hand. In Fred's vision, divorced from reality, everyone in the world knew the Bradys were a musical family act much like the Von Trapp family minus the nuns and the Nazis. They were so successful they had landed their own TV series, just like the Osmonds, and they had moved from their house in an unnamed Los Angeles suburb to a swell place at the beach where they had a huge swimming pool conveniently located right next to the ocean. Every day they headed into Hollywood and worked on their television show. The stories would revolve around how they lived their Brady lives and did their Brady show, peppered with whatever guest stars happened to be on the show that week.

The stars would not only work on the Brady show, they would somehow insinuate themselves into the Bradys' lives. This had worked years ago for Jack Benny.* But there was only one Benny and there were eight Bradys. So I'm sure Fred felt he had at least sixteen legs up on Jack.

Armed with a recommendation from Florence, I got the job. But the real reason was I had just done, with Florence, that *Paul Lynde Halloween Special* you may recently have read about. One of the guest stars on that show was Billie Hayes in her character of Witchiepoo, a creation of Sid and Marty Krofft, about whom you also may recently have read. We had such a good time on that show that they asked me to come on this one. It is important that you have a good time. At least it was in the '70s, and especially with Sid and Marty, who, as Warren Beatty said of Jack Nicholson when he gave him the AFI Life Achievement Award, were guys who would go to great lengths to have a good time.

The Kroffts were limited in what they could do on Paul's special—they were just there babysitting their character—but as executive producers on the Brady show, they would have free rein. So everyone else had to hold on.

If you saw a picture of the writers' room they assembled and you're a card-carrying wokester, you would go into full-bore apoplexy. Everybody was White and male. But that was just for the picture.

---

* Benjamin Kubelsky from Waukegan, Illinois, became Jack Benny, a fiddle-playing comedian who was a smash in vaudeville, on radio, and finally on television, as well as in a few movies. His carefully curated character was a notorious cheapskate who told us he was thirty-nine for at least four decades after he was. Jack's TV show was about him doing a TV show every week and alternated between his home in Beverly Hills, where he had a wife and a chauffeur (Eddie "Rochester" Anderson), and the studio, where he had an announcer and a boyish tenor who sang on the show. Guest stars, including Marilyn Monroe, would appear both at the house and in the studio. Jack might not have invented the deadpan reaction, but he perfected it and has influenced every comic actor on the planet.

In reality, it was six degrees of diversity. Gay, straight, druggy, sober, very druggy, longtime married, short-time married several times, straight-becoming-gay . . . It was almost like one of those WWII bomber crew movies, except for the gay stuff.

Ronny Graham loped over from the Paul Lynde show with me, and we were joined by a very high-energy writer named Mike Kagan, very bright and full of ideas, neither of which was even a minimal requirement for this show.

Sitting on the couch and looking gorgeous was Terry Hart, who could easily have stepped in for a young Sam Elliott in that movie about lifeguards, but who chose instead to write for Johnny Carson and a dozen sitcoms that actually were funny. It's very rare to find a beautiful comedy writer of any of the many sexes now on offer. I spent a lot of time staring at him and dropping pencils in his vicinity.

Then there was Steve Bluestein, stand-up, author, and liver of a life of endless drama, which he would tell you about every morning until you had to be helped to the recovery room to get something that made you stop laughing. Steve got a nose job and a divorce in the two or three months we spent working on *The Brady Bunch Hour*, and that was just for starters. We have remained friends and the Sturm und Drang never stops, nor do the laughs.

Marshaling these troops was a fantastically funny guy named Carl Kleinschmitt, a dream boss and collaborator who later wrote one of my favorite comedies of the period, a picture called *Middle Age Crazy* (1980), worth checking out. He was boyish, bell-bottomed, and deceptively hippie-ish, but equipped with a sharp mind and razor wit.

Among his many talents, Carl was an inspired practical joker, and on the Brady show, he pulled off a classic that was both hilarious and obscene, meaning it would still get bleeped today, maybe even on Pornhub.

Carl's agent at the time was a young upstart at the William Morris Agency named Mike Ovitz. You may have heard of him. Some months after the incident to be described, he and a few other young upstarts left Morris and founded Creative Artists Agency, CAA, the dominant agency in town to this day, unless Godzilla has come over from Japan and stomped on their building while I wasn't looking. Godzilla, by the way, is a client.

From CAA, Mike, who became Michael somewhere along the line, went to Disney, where he endured a short, much-maligned reign that resulted in one of the more brilliantly golden parachutes ever deployed. He then became an art collector with a house at the beach even sweller than the Bradys'.

At the time of our story, he was an eager wheeler-dealer who actually represented a comedy writer on a variety show. OK, a *head* writer, but still, this is a far cry from negotiating sales of entire studios and all the other stuff he did later. He was also a big fan of Marie Osmond. We were taping the pilot of the Brady series, and the Kroffts, who also had *Donny & Marie* on the air and on the same studio lot, had gotten the Osmonds to guest. The Brady kids had done a guest shot on their show a few weeks earlier as a clever promotional tool.

This was our first show—at the time I don't think we knew if there would be a second—and for that reason everyone's support troops showed up, and by that I mean their agents and parents. And some of their agents' parents, because it was *The Brady Bunch*.

Donny and Marie were huge stars at that point, but they were kids—Marie was actually underage—and they lived in a bubble of family, religion, and work, surrounded by minders. Because they were pursued by paparazzi and by fans, they each had doubles, people who looked like them and were used as decoys. The doubles would leave by the front door, the singles by the back, and so forth.

Marie's double looked startlingly like Marie. She was older, legal in fact, but when in her working makeup and attire a dead ringer, with the same open, sunny smile. She was a smart young woman with a genuine sense of humor about her work and had been around show business long enough that nothing fazed her. She would drop in on the writers every now and again and we would share some off-color laughs with her. A perfect partner in practical joke crime.

As rehearsals progressed onstage, I noticed Carl huddling with her in the corner. After a little while, Mike Ovitz arrived with two or three other Morrismen, as the trade papers used to call them. Carl and the double walked over to welcome them. Mike's eyes lit up. He thought it was Marie. Carl did the introductions, Mike said something charming, and the double smiled that identical Marie smile and said, "Oh, Mr. Ovitz. I've heard so much about you." Mike smiled a bit sheepishly. "Yes," she continued, "I would like you to come to my dressing room *(slight pause)* so I can make you come on my teeth."

There was a stunned silence, somewhat like the moment in atomic bomb test films when the explosion occurs and the mushroom cloud appears but you haven't heard anything yet. Everyone just froze. And then, in gangster-movie parlance, the dime dropped and everyone got it at once. This was not Marie Osmond, this was not anything Marie Osmond would ever say, yet it was occurring in real time. The single most hilarious and obscene example of what can happen when preparation meets opportunity. And I told you it was obscene. But isn't that what you've always thought about Hollywood?

It took us a while to work up to this particular moment. A month, in fact. When we all gathered in Carl's office for the first time, it never occurred to any of us that we would become such degenerates in such a short time. After all, this was the Brady Bunch, spotless and virginal, yet it was about to become the proverbially sunny show written by shady people. None of us had worked on the old Brady show. That was very much a family affair lorded over by Sherwood Schwartz, the man who created the weirdly trippy *Gilligan's Island* in the '60s, just *before* hallucinogens had gotten on the scene, although that show certainly had the whiff of wacky weed about it.

Sherwood had retreated from that island into milky-White suburbia with the Bradys. Not only had we not written for the original show, I doubt that any of us actually ever watched it. I was working as an entertainment writer at the *Chicago Tribune* when the show premiered, but I reviewed something else that night. One rare Friday evening when I was at home at 7:00 central and still in my right mind, I think I watched an episode just to see what it was all about. It was nothing I would otherwise have tuned in to. Since I was not alone in having the Bradys in my blind spot, some of the newly hired scribes spent a few hours huddled around a videotape player boning up.

The gloom that followed was broken when we realized that our show had taken an existential leap, if I can use that phrase in the same sentence as the words *Brady Bunch*. This was not another episode of the old show, this was a new show in which the Bradys themselves were not San Fernando Valley locals but TV stars surrounded by chorus girls and other TV stars pretending to be themselves, when they weren't in sketches pretending to be even more ridiculous characters. Why we thought we could pull that off is one of the minor questions still floating about the universe. Fred Silverman thought we could. The only other answer was . . . why not? It was in that pioneer spirit that we plunged into whatever this was going to be.

One thing a weekly variety show has to be is funny, and not the kind of sweet, antiseptic funny that is the neighborhood where a family sitcom lives. Sherwood Schwartz appreciated this when he cast the one non-Brady element in his original show: Ann B. Davis as Alice, the Bradys' maid. I adored her when I was a kid, as most of the country did when she appeared as Schultzy, Bob Cummings's man-hungry secretary on his eponymous sitcom, sometimes known as *Love That Bob* (1955–1959). Sherwood was clearly looking for that same dry but zany timing from Ann B., but he toned her down a bit when he created Alice. She wasn't so much man hungry as man attentive, and then it was only toward one man, Sam the butcher, and their romance was as nonspecific as a romance can be. She also abandoned the withering put-downs for good-natured ribbing. On the original Brady show, that was about as adult as things got. Earnestness was in abundance; grown-up comedy was not. Not that what we were contemplating for Alice was anything too grown-up. But the family *was* living in Malibu and *was* working in show business, so there had to be some concessions made.

Plus, the original show was shot like a movie, on film, with no audience and a laugh track. Our show, brilliantly lit on tape, was going to look like a stage musical, and although the laugh track would be yukking it up, there would be a live audience for the finale in all its Vegas spectacle. So the performance energy was going to be a lot different, and the Bradys, en famille, did not have that kind of punch. Why would they? Even Ann B., an experienced stage comedienne who had done musicals all over the country and on Broadway, where she followed Carol Burnett into the original production of *Once Upon a Mattress* in 1960, was playing a low-energy character who commented on everything that was going on. So the call went out for another new character for her to play off of, someone who would be flat-out funny and perhaps a bit over the top, to bring things from simmer to boil. And that would be Rip Taylor.

Rip, who emerged periodically from a vat of confetti to play Vegas, tour in musicals, judge contestants on *The Gong Show*, and generally wreak havoc wherever he went, was exactly the tonic that was needed. Just putting him in the same room as the Bradys was hilarious. In the great tradition of situation comedy, we made him the next-door neighbor so he could burst upon the scene at any moment with whatever farkakte plot device we needed him for. He could also be our Sam the butcher, if Alice could actually pretend to be interested in him.

This proved to be more difficult than we envisioned. Ann B. had found Jesus and was living in a religious community to which she returned every weekend. She had no interest in giving Alice an interior life that involved a dalliance with Rip Taylor. She also didn't care for Rip personally. He was a real people pleaser, but he was all over the place and always in your face, and she was having none of it. She had a great relationship with all the Bradys. They had been a family, after all, for years. But she got no pleasure out of our new baby. I frankly don't know what she got real pleasure out of, although I had my suspicions. We had a great relationship. She viewed me as an odd duck, but a nonthreatening one, and we talked a lot about her experience in the early days of television until she would get too deep into an anecdote and suddenly remember she had found Jesus and whatever we were talking about was something we shouldn't be talking about. Rip, who lived to please, was frustrated beyond words with her attitude, but she was pretty implacable. He would bring her donuts, he would write her notes, he would throw his toupee in her lap and cry "Small rug alert!" Nuttin', honey.

One of the things that became apparent once we spent time with the cast, adults and kids, was that none of them, with the exception of old pro Florence, knew exactly what the show was going to be. To be fair, we didn't either, but we had at least been told in rough terms. According to the cast, they all thought they were going into some sort of revival of the old show with some musical element added. They didn't think they were expected to become Osmonds overnight, that there would be songs to learn, dance routines to master, characters to play in sketches. And the characters wouldn't simply be characters. They would be their Brady character *playing* a character. Suddenly, each of them had to become Pirandello, working on several levels. This was a drastic change from entering from the backyard and asking Alice what was for dinner.

Robert Reed, the captain of the SS *Brady*, was especially hard hit by this revelation, as he was a seriously serious actor. Which is not to say he was a Method guy desperately searching for the brooch in the drapes (one of Stanislavski's famous exercises). He had started as a wonderful light comedian, following Robert Redford in the Neil Simon smash hit *Barefoot in the Park* on Broadway in 1964. But he had made his bones on a highly regarded courtroom drama, *The Defenders* (1961–1965). He had wound up in Bradyland by circumstance. Now he was going to have to figure out how to be the stolid, upstanding dad playing goofy characters in sketches and, even more daunting, being a song-and-dance man. If you ever watch the show, you will see a man going through a deep psychological struggle trying to make sense of Mike Brady, architect and family man, attempting a soft-shoe with a straw hat and cane. Every number was like talent night at the Moose Lodge.

Bob was extremely closeted. So was Rip, but nothing Rip did was ever real, so the matter never came up; Bob lived in abject terror that he would be revealed. I thought this might give him a great excuse to let his frustrations out by being over the top when the performance called for it—as it did almost every week—but he didn't see it that way. A few years later, I saw him on Broadway, where he was one of the many actors who stepped into *Deathtrap* during its marathon run from 1978 to 1982. Afterward, he told me he was enjoying it, but it wasn't as much fun as the variety hour. I thought he was joking. I can't ever recall *him* having fun, although I guess it became his official story after a while. Except . . . there was one time when he might have been channeling some inner amusement. It was when we all held our breath and put him in drag as Carmen Miranda.*

Yes, we did. Fruit basket on the head and everything. It must have been for a finale, and he had an audience to play to. The congas and the maracas must have freed him, as they have many men, to discover

---

* Carmen Miranda was a petite ball of energy from Brazil who could sing and dance and balance forty pounds of fruit on her head while doing the first two, and in platform heels. If you haven't seen her, you've seen someone who has seen her and has appropriated her act. She was a huge addition to any movie musical of the '40s. Charo is the closest thing to Carmen still active today, but her act is much more overtly sexual. *Cuchi-cuchi* is all hers.

their inner *cuchi-cuchi*. Getting into the costume was no easy trick. First of all, *getting* the costume was no easy trick. Our designer, Pete Menefee, a former dancer whose ideas prefigured *Priscilla, Queen of the Desert*, was in the middle of a budget crunch, so he scoured the town for Carmen Miranda drag, knowing that every costume house had a bunch of them squirreled away. Of course, they were not all in Bob's size. But one of them was. It was in storage over the hill at NBC in Burbank, and he raced over before anyone could get it and raced back, chuckling all the way because the label in it indicated it was made for Toni Tennille. She's a tall girl. He was chuckling away when he was pulled over for speeding.

Frantic, he blurted out to the cop that he had to get this dress to the KTLA studio, his job was on the line, and please let him go. The cop was intrigued. "Who's it for?" he asked. "Robert Reed," Pete replied hysterically. The cop gave him a look. "The dad on *The Brady Bunch*?" he asked. Pete shrieked "Yes!" A moment passed. The cop said, "Hey, this is Hollywood. You couldn't make this shit up. Get going!" And Pete got gone.

Bob made a fabulous lady in the tutti-frutti hat—better than Toni Tennille, I betcha. It was quite a performance. He was Mike Brady dressed as Carmen Miranda. All the apprehension Bob had and all the fun he was having, for once, playing dress-up coalesced into something that had to be seen.

Toni Tennille's wardrobe made another secret appearance on the show. Again, during budget-crunch time, Pete found a terrific dress for Tina Turner, who was guesting on the show and doing a solo. This was just after Tina ran away from Ike and before her renaissance began with her cover of Al Green's "Let's Stay Together" in 1983. She'd left everything when she left Ike, and she needed a dress. Pete found a gold lamé mini that showed off her legs, pretty spectacular, but after the rehearsal she came over and said the edge of the armhole, called the armscye, was cutting into her flesh. "I don't know who you made this for, but she must have been a much taller girl," she said conspiratorially. You guessed it. That other TT.

If I remember correctly, Tina did her solo on the stage around the water tank. The Osmonds next door had an ice rink, and Sid Krofft thought it would be good for the Bradys to have a water ballet. Every week. So the Krofftettes became a synchronized swimming act, doing kicklines in the pool with lots of overhead shots of their geometrical formations. Nobody else was doing this sort of thing, and we found out why. It was a pain in the ass to put together every week. This was not MGM in the '40s with a unit devoted to Esther Williams pictures.* Even though it was a tortuous process, the crew was very happy working on the numbers, largely because the tank was built up off the stage floor and had portholes all around it so the cameras could do underwater shots. The numbers were rehearsed endlessly, and if you were looking for a particular crew or cast member who wasn't where he was supposed to be, he was generally glued to a porthole watching the lower half of the Krofftettes and hoping for a breaststroke. Ronny Graham was often found there, and some guest stars had to be pried off the portholes like squid.

Guest stars were a problem, because the show hadn't established itself as a good showcase for them, so the network executive ABC assigned to the show, a classy blonde dynamo with the patience of saints and angels named Bonny Dore, spent hours cajoling everyone's agent, manager, hairstylist, holistic pet psychiatrist, or BFF of the moment to get someone on the show. As a result, we had some pretty bizarre guests, like Tina (with the Brady Bunch? Really?), and some show business veterans like Edgar Bergen, Milton Berle, Charo (already a veteran), and my personal favorite, Vincent Price.

---

* Esther Williams was a champion swimmer who became one of the biggest movie personalities of the 1940s and '50s. She was a surprisingly skilled comic actress who had a way with a wisecrack, and she could sing and dance, and boy could she dive.

What do you do with Vincent Price and the Brady Bunch? This was before he contributed the spooky narration to Michael Jackson's "Thriller" (1982), but Vincent, who had started as a character actor and occasional leading man and had segued into cheesy self-parody horror flicks, was already a camp figure and leaning into it. He came to the set with his wife, Coral Browne, particularly remembered these days for playing Auntie Mame's diva friend Vera Charles, which was an extension of her own theatrical personality. She had a wicked wit— they both did—and their bemusement at being surrounded by all this wholesomeness was a show in itself. But what to do with Vincent?

Each week we had a Brady story that threaded through the show in between the musical numbers. We were aware that a lot of our audience had followed the family through all of the seasons of the old show. Our kids were older now and needed stories that reflected that. So we decided it would be a good time to let Greg rebel, break away from the homestead, and with his newfound TV salary, get himself his own apartment. Rip, ever the solicitous next-door neighbor, accompanies him to make sure nobody takes advantage of the kid. He hasn't got that much money to spend, so he winds up looking at a pretty funky pad, as they were known then. While he's inspecting it, Vincent Price arrives.

He may have been there already, we can't be sure. He's ghost hunting, as Vincent Price does of a weekend. I thought he should be looking for a ghost named Stella. This would allow him to stalk through the apartment crying "STELLA!" in a Vincent Price impression of Marlon Brando. Trust me, back then it still registered. Well, Stella isn't around, but it occurs to Vincent that Greg Brady might be the ghost. There are several he's been looking for, and Greg might be Binkie Beaumont, or Kitty Sheehan, or Zelda Makowsky, or her dog Pickles. These were all names I put in the script that Vincent found hilarious and went along with. Binkie Beaumont was a very flamboyant stage producer in London, and Coral Browne had worked for him, as had everyone else. Kitty Sheehan was for my friends in Chicago. She was a crusty old lesbian who ran a bar with her own name that was populated entirely by ancient queens, to the point that people around town called it the "wrinkle room." Kitty was a dead ringer for Mayor Richard J. Daley—and, in fact, they never were seen together. Zelda Makowsky played cards with my mother in Paterson, New Jersey, and Pickles was her dachshund who was such a purebred he could actually fart "Deutschland Über Alles."

Amazingly, the sketch went very well. Vincent scares the shite out of Greg and has him scurrying back into the bosom of the Bradys. We did it in a couple of takes that had to be stopped because we were all laughing, and when it was through, Rip stopped everything before we moved on and said, "I think we'd all like to thank the writers." Of course, we thought it was a joke, but he was being totally sincere. And Vincent Price said, "Hear hear!" and, for a minute, we all thought we were pretty hot shite. But it wore off soon enough and we got back to business.

When Milton Berle was on the show, our business was establishing whether or not the famous rumor about the comedian was true: that he had the largest penis in Hollywood. We were having a casual reading of his material with him in the writers' room and he announced he had to use the men's room. He got up and left. We all looked at each other. We all got up and headed for the men's room. It was standing room only in there. It often is in a men's room, but not for this reason. Milton looked around and we were waiting for him to laugh, but he didn't. He just looked puzzled. So the group got out of there, but not before I boldly went where no man had gone before and said, "I just want to see it." Milton said, "Why? Are you queer?" I said, "That's beside the point. I want to see something Marilyn Monroe saw."

Milton was well known for telling people he had had an affair with Marilyn. This surprised no one, as Marilyn Monroe was known to have had an affair or two with famous men. I was sure Milton had been hit on, but probably no one had ever done it this way. He laughed and said, "Let's get back to work before I call your mother."

I got to know him a little better over the years, but I never got what Marilyn got. And it turns out Milton actually *knew* my mother. His wife, Ruth, was from Paterson, where she did not play cards with Zelda Makowsky but did know my family. I wonder if he actually knew what he was threatening.

I was never certain if Robert Reed was having a good time, but I knew the rest of us were. At least half of the Brady kids have written memoirs telling us exactly how good a time they were having, with and without chemical additives.

Florence was having a great time, and we were having a great time with her. As production went on, a lot of people around the show who only knew her as Carol Brady, world champion homemaker, were beginning to discover the other side of Florence. One day, an interviewer from the *New York Times*, or maybe the *Los Angeles Times*, or

When a Hells Angel comes to *The Brady Bunch Hour*, Florence is shocked by the authentic casting.

it could have been *Time* magazine—they all showed up at one time or another—was sequestered with Florence in her dressing room at lunch.

We decided it was time to let Florence's freak flag fly. I started by going into her room—she had foolishly left the door open—and instantly apologized for interrupting the interview. As I left, I casually turned and said, "Florence, whatever you do, don't mention the acid-throwing incident." She laughed and I went out. A few minutes later, another member of the writing staff did exactly the same thing. When the third member of the staff came in, the reporter said, "All right, tell me about the acid-throwing incident," to which Florence replied with a laugh, "There was no acid-throwing incident." The reporter looked at her dubiously. "You deny the acid-throwing incident?" Ronny Graham then walked in and said, "For Chrissake, Florence, don't talk about the acid-throwing incident." Then to the reporter, "The acid-throwing is strictly off the record. Not only that, it's on background. Deep background. In fact, it's classified." The reporter looked at Florence and said, "Does this go on every day on *The Brady Bunch*?" "This is chump change," Florence replied. "You've no idea."

Unsullied by our prank, Florence made a quick appearance the next day in the doorway of the writers' room, cleared her throat, flashed her boobs, and continued down the hall.

Some of us were hoping the interview would demonstrate that the show was getting a bit more colorful, but for some reason it was never published. The press thought the show was ridiculous, and it was difficult to prove them wrong. It was what it was, an attempt to shoehorn one specific format into another. Those never work; they just confuse audiences, because they have to serve too many masters. Lots of bad shows *have* survived, of course, but none of them had the added burden of being on a wheel.

I beg your pardon? Certainly. A wheel was a programming concept that had a vogue in the '70s. It was where you programmed several different shows in rotation in the same time period each week. NBC's Sunday Mystery Movie was a successful wheel, with *Columbo*, *McMillan & Wife*, *McCloud*, and a few others. Those shows were each ninety-minute movies, and having to make fewer of them per season meant the creatives could spend more time on each one. It helped that they were all mysteries.

The Bradys, thought to appeal to a younger audience, were on a wheel with . . . two mysteries, also thought to appeal to a younger audience: *The Hardy Boys* and *Nancy Drew*. So our hour only showed up once every three weeks, if that. Between preemptions for specials, we only had to do nine shows. Other than the fact that we had young kids, none of whom were stars, we had nothing in common with the two mystery shows. *The Hardy Boys* caught on immediately—Shaun Cassidy was one of them—and the network began ordering up more episodes of that, so we showed up maybe once a month on what was now beginning to resemble a torture wheel. The audience never got a chance to develop the habit of watching us. Each time they tuned in, they were rediscovering what a bizarre concept the show was, and each time the press had a chance to look aghast at what we were trying to do.

In the spring of 1977, the poor child was finally put to rest. Or so we thought. The Bradys continued on with shows about Brady kids, about Brady brides, about Brady reunions, but nothing attempting to do what we did. The Schwartz dynasty reclaimed the brand and went back to slightly more modern versions of the old show. And eventually, in what was either hubris or a very shrewd move, Paramount made *The Brady Bunch Movie* (1995), but it was a parody of the original show, almost as if the crew behind *Airplane!* and *The Naked Gun* had been let loose on it. It was a surprise hit and spawned a sequel, but in the immediate aftermath, everything Brady got a rebirth, including us. There we were, back on TV—Nick at Nite, no less—in our confetti-stained glory. And a whole generation that never knew we existed could suddenly wallow in our infamy.

So it was one afternoon when I was sitting at my desk, working on something much more grown-up, that I got a call from a young stoner friend of mine. "Dude!" he began, "I was up in the middle of the night and turned on the TV looking for *SpongeBob* and there was, on my TV, the dad from *The Brady Bunch* and he had a fruit basket on his head and he was doing some kind of *cuchi-cuchi* Charo dance. And the credits rolled and your name was on it! WTF? How did *that* happen?"

Dude, go back to the top of this chapter.

4

The Ice Pirates (1984)

Or, at Least the Space Herpe Didn't Have Lines

Contrary to what the previous chapters may have led you to believe, all the bad ideas in the world did not stem from variety television shows. Some of them came from the Hollywood studios: big-screen disasters whose horrible reputations have outlived even those of accomplished dictators of medium-sized countries.

The next disaster in which I was a willing accomplice was actually a half-assed hit. At least, that was what the producer called it when he phoned me Monday morning when the opening-weekend box-office numbers came out. This was in 1984—the real one, not the Orwellian fiction—back when you didn't know by end of business on Friday whether or not you could show your face at the restaurant of the moment on Monday. The picture was called *The Ice Pirates*.

It wasn't called that originally. What picture would be called that originally? Originally it was called *The Water Planet*, something Kevin Costner, Guillermo del Toro, or James Cameron never would have called any of *their* water movies. But then, the first script, from a man who had written a picture called *Krull* (1983), was a dead-serious sci-fi action-adventure.

Stanford Sherman wrote of a heavily populated space-faring universe where water was the most precious commodity, harvested on planets that had it, then frozen and shipped to planets that didn't. Marauding bands of cutthroats hijacked the intergalactic ships and stole the frozen water. They were known as ice pirates. Makes sense so far. A little unwieldy, transferring all those giant ice cubes from one spaceship to another, but still.

The script caught the eye of a formidable producer named John Foreman. John was a fabulous Hollywood character: elegant, a bit epicene, and a lot intellectual. We had great fun at dinners rolling our eyes at some of the folk we in our perceived eminence deemed parvenus. John's producing career began with a picture called *Winning* (1969), which was made to cater to Paul Newman's obsession with Formula One and stock car racing and anything with a stick shift that could go from 0 to 100 in nanoseconds. It costarred Paul's wife, Joanne Woodward, one of the most brilliant actresses ever, who often took roles in Paul's movies so she could keep an eye on him. John and Paul formed a deep professional friendship that carried them through many movies, though their second collaboration is the most notable: *Butch Cassidy and the Sundance Kid* (1969), for which John got an Oscar nomination (Best Picture). Their company was Newman-Foreman, and it had an office on the MGM lot in Culver City.

By the early '80s, Metro-Goldwyn-Mayer had fallen from the Promethean heights of Hollywood's golden age to a much smaller, financially strapped, undernourished lion king. The studio was now suffering the whip of David Begelman, a jovial crook who had once managed Judy Garland and evidently had emotional problems, which led him to mess around with the studio's finances and his checkbook.

As a studio head, he knew there was an upside to a movie like *The Water Planet*. Big-budget science fiction had recently come back in style with *Star Wars*. The *Water Planet* script had caught John Foreman's eye not because he was passionate about sci-fi but because the antihero, a Harrison Ford–ish character who was the leader of a pirate gang, looked like a good fit for Robert Urich.

As it happens, I knew Bob Urich from my Chicago journalism days, when he and his wife, Heather, who had played one of the Von Trapp kids in the film version of *The Sound of Music* (1965), were local actors who showed up in a lot of stage productions around town. One of them was a production of *The Rainmaker*, N. Richard Nash's 1954 Broadway hit that became a big movie for Burt Lancaster and Katharine Hepburn two years later—not to be confused with the John Grisham novel, totally different, that came later. The 1972 Chicago show starred Burt Reynolds and Lois Nettleton and featured a handsome young guy named Bob Urich.

Reynolds saw something of himself in Bob, so he got his agent to take him on, and soon Bob was in Hollywood, doing lots of TV guest shots and pilots and, at length, hitting on one that scored big: *Vega$* (1978–1981)—yes, with a dollar sign. Bob played a private eye in, where else, Oy Vegas, and in a lovely inside joke, he was named Dan Tanna after famous restaurateur Dan Tana, whose West Hollywood namesake place is still a show biz hot spot. Dan Tanna solved crimes in his red '57 T-bird, crimes that often involved buxom showgirls.

After three seasons, *Vega$* lost its dollar sign and its time slot, but there is always room for a hunk who can do action and comedy, and another show, *Gavilan* (1982–1983), surfaced. And *surfaced* is the appropriate term, for in this one Bob played a former CIA agent turned oceanographer who gets into the most goldarn adventures.

Gavilan sank to the bottom after ten episodes, but it didn't matter for Bob. As enticement to get him to do the show, the producers— MGM's TV division—threw in a promise to develop movies for him. The first was a bizarre item—if you think *The Ice Pirates* is bizarre, wait till you get a load of this—titled *Endangered Species* (1982). It opens with a cow that fell out of a helicopter. The cow was dead long before she got on the chopper, the victim of a lab-leaked bug, and Bob is a former New York City cop passing through town who helps the local authorities clean up the mess. In hindsight, with Wuhan and nightmare variants and climate control clearly in our frame of reference, the movie was fairly prescient. At the time, it was a movie that most people thought was about a recent, mysterious string of supposed cow mutilations, but like the old folks say, you never can tell. Hit or miss, Metro was obligated to come up with more projects for Bob.

John Foreman cannily saw how *The Water Planet* could solve a few problems for the studio by marrying their TV star to a big sci-fi epic, but one that didn't take itself quite so seriously. And was not about cows. The pirate hero also appealed to Bob, who was eager to swash a buckle like Burt Lancaster and, before him, Errol Flynn and, come to think of it, Harrison Ford. So Bob was in. Once that happened, all things made sense.

There was still the question of budget. *The Water Planet* was to be a $20-million picture, which today is the rock-bottom figure a big-name star will accept for making a movie. At the time, it was considered a sizable investment for a studio, especially one as cash starved as MGM. Its bankers didn't see the efficacy of making it for that much money. They thought it would come in just fine at $8 million, which today is the rock-bottom figure a big-name star's hairdresser will accept for making a movie.

They weren't trying to bury the project. They thought *no* picture should cost more than $8 million. How they arrived at that figure is an actuary's wet dream, and I still wonder if, had we progressed into algorithms, we might have gotten a bit more, but $8 million it was. So John decided that if the film leaned more on the comedy than on big-boom effects and glitzy hardware, it might get away with being something rare: a funny action-adventure movie with a sort of homemade quality.

To achieve this, he took the Sherman script and sent it to Stewart Raffill, an affable British director who had made a picture called *High Risk* (1981), which was something along the lines of what John had in mind. Stewart had a rough-and-tumble pioneer comedy sense, and he saw the water planet as a romp, not something that would ever become the food of the nerds. He proceeded to rewrite the script according to that guiding principle. And he retitled it *The Ice Pirates*.

Among his concoctions was a wicked emperor, or an emperor who thinks he's wicked but is actually a man-child still slave to his infantile impulses. In his original state he was small and adorable, so he was of course offered to Paul Williams, who accepted.* Emperor Wendon, or Weird Wendon, as he is frequently referred to, is a compulsive gambler who has—prepare yourself, this is a stretch—gambled away parts of his body in what must have been a *very* high-stakes game. In fact, he has lost his entire body; all that's left is his head, and thanks to the miracle of robot technology, he lives on as a series of bodies wherever he can get somebody to hook him up. This is what owning a Roomba will lead you to. If you think *that* concept is bizarre, Stewart also invented a monster to crawl around the ship called a Space Herpe. Wormlike and glistening, it's not something you want to be petting.

These additions proved to be indispensable to the legend of *The Ice Pirates*. A few weeks before production was scheduled to begin, several interesting things happened. It was decided by one and all that the script, now a comedy, needed to have some funny lines to match the absurd situations that Stewart had cooked up. So John called me and asked me to come in and do a little fluffing.

---

* Paul Williams was, dare I say it, the Peter Dinklage of his day. Not really an actor, Paul is a singer-songwriter who collaborated with Barbra Streisand on her song "Evergreen" for *A Star Is Born* (1976) and with the very much taller Pat McCormick in several Burt Reynolds movies in which they were a comic duo. He had a terrific concert career and he actually is not a little person but a short person, but one with a real reason to live. I have been called, physically, a Maxi-Paul.

I was delighted. I got to spend time with Bob Urich and John, and I loved Stewart and we laughed a lot. And then the next interesting thing happened. Paul Williams quit. I was never sure why, but I walked in one day and John and Stewart said, "Good morning, Weird Wendon." My Screen Actors Guild health insurance prospects looked a lot brighter.

I went about adjusting the script, removing the "short" jokes—that was what they did with Paul Williams back then—and finding things for Wendon to do. I showed them my fixes and John said, "We don't see him coming in on page 3. The picture is not about him. He doesn't show up till page 44."

OK, sue me, I tried. I downsized myself, not to Paul's size—not even Ozempic could do that—but so that the part was now a flavor in the cauldron. Wendon showed up when they needed a quick laugh, and the best part, he was almost always seated because his body was never his own. When he didn't have a host and was existing as a head in the wild, I would spend a lot of time crammed into furniture with my noggin sticking out, but it was a small price to pay.

We continued writing, fixing, laughing, and having lunch in the legendary MGM commissary, the Lion's Den—I think the inner sanctum was called the Cub Room—and then one day, driving from my house in Laurel Canyon to Culver City, a thing happened that was so interesting that it made all the earlier interesting things look positively drab. David Begelman was fired.

And John Foreman was made head of MGM. And he immediately greenlit *The Ice Pirates*. And we had a start date. And this was before I finished the bagel I was munching on the way to work.

John moved from his production office in a small adobe structure to the sprawling office originally occupied by Louis B. Mayer in a corner of the Irving Thalberg Building, and we had a good chuckle over how he was perhaps the least legendary person to plant his cheeks on the swivel chair behind a desk the size of Nevada.

There wasn't as much time to schmooze, as he now had a studio to run, although *The Ice Pirates* was the only project ready to roll. John had to get busy casting it. I mean, there were other parts besides Bob's pirate hero and my Weird Wendon, if you can believe it.

People always assume that anybody casting a legitimate Hollywood project has their choice of just about any actor in the world, but the grim truth is that once you consider every prospect's level of fame, price point, suitability for the role, availability for when you need them, past relationships with other people in the cast and crew, marketability outside the United States, and, oh yes, whether or not they have any desire at all to play this particular part, you often find that you are staring into a very shallow pool. You can't always get what you want, but if you try real hard, you might get what you need. This should have been a sampler on John's wall when it came to casting our little fantasy.

One day he told me to meet him in one of the intimate screening rooms on the lot, where we settled in to watch a picture called *A Walk with Love and Death* (1969). Didn't sound like it would be a riotous morning, but Woody Allen had made a picture called *Love and Death* that was very funny, and besides love and death, this one also had a walk.

It also had a peasant rebellion that happened in France in 1358, during which a medieval romance bloomed in between beheadings and pig-slopping. The lovers were played by two children of famous men: Assaf Dayan, whose father was the legendary Israeli warrior Moshe Dayan, and Anjelica Huston, whose father was the legendary Hollywood warrior John Huston, also the director of the picture, and a supporting player.

This was the young lovers' first movie. Assaf, who for unfathomable reasons later changed his name to Assi, would never find international success, remaining an actor and director in Israel. Anjelica, who was still a teenager at the time, had been slated to play Juliet for Franco Zeffirelli in his famously lusty version of Shakespeare but was pulled out of that production by her father to do this one. She didn't look thrilled about any of it, but she had, as they say, "a quality." Her strong angular looks held the screen, and she had a powerful personal presence.

"I think she'd be good for the Amazon pirate," John said. I didn't know there *was* an Amazon pirate, and I was working on the script. Then I realized that, yes, there was a female pirate, and she could be a warrior, but she wasn't terribly funny.

And that turned out to be Anjelica's long suit: she could play deadpan, but with a suggestion of some sort of mischief under the surface. I thought she would play the hell out of that pirate without even trying, and with the boots we were planning to strap her into, she would give us Amazon Plus. I also knew that John Foreman and John Huston were old friends, and Foreman probably knew Anjelica from her childhood. What I didn't know was that the two Johns were in development on a movie called *Prizzi's Honor*, a human-interest gangster picture, which doesn't make any sense until you see it. John Foreman had a plan.

The other big female part in our epic was cast with the daughter of another famous man and friend of John's, Mary Crosby, known as Mary Frances Crosby when she appeared as part of the cheery family Christmas portrait on her dad Bing Crosby's TV specials.

More recently, she was known as the girl who shot J. R. That would be J. R. Ewing, the dastardly villain of *Dallas*, the prime-time soap that captivated America in the late '70s. The show's mass hysteria high point in 1980 was one of the great cliffhangers of all time, as season 3 ends with J. R. Ewing being shot by an unseen assailant. Next fall, it's revealed that it was Mary what done it. She then left the show, but movie stardom had not yet beckoned, and, crazy as it sounded, our little venture might put her over the top. Look what *Star Wars* had done for Carrie Fisher. So Mary was our princess in flowing white and the love interest for Bob Urich, who didn't seem to mind one bit.

Anjelica got a love interest, too: the mountainous John Matuszak, the football player, who played the pirate who got the Amazon. John was *not* a friend of John's, but he was a friend of a friend of John's who was partially financing the picture, and it was suggested by said friend that in a picture called *The Ice Pirates*, there *had* to be a part for a survivor of the NFL, or at least the National Hockey League. Tooz, as he liked to be called, had acted before in a very good Nick Nolte comedy called *North Dallas Forty* (1979) in which they both played . . . football players. And he also held forth with Ringo Starr—yes, him—in a picture called *Caveman* (1981) in which they played . . . don't think too much about it.

Tooz was great fun the way you hope athletes will be great fun: warm, engaging, unflappable. It's no secret that he was a top-tier partyer, the grim facts of which were revealed in the coroner's report when he died ridiculously young in 1989.

There were days when you could tell there was some sort of chemical alteration happening. It came to a head one afternoon when he streaked off the lot in his hot convertible for a lunch date and plowed into a lamppost. We all ran out to see if he was all right. I had to extricate myself from a table—I was bodyless by then—and by the time I got there ambulances and paramedics were at work and a lot of people in strange space-age costumes were hovering around him. He was a little banged up but returned the next day, as I recall, and shrugged it off the way athletes do. An old MGM hand mumbled to me that this was the same lamppost that Van Johnson had driven into in the late '40s, resulting in a scar that you can still see in some of his movies. I know that sounds like dialogue from *Sunset Blvd.*, and believe me, that was exactly what I was thinking as the old-timer was telling me. But that stuff really happens.

Another pirate on our team was also fresh from a triumph as a caveman, Ron Perlman, who went from being a character actor to being a character star. He had just done *Quest for Fire* (1981), the very artsy caveman movie—as opposed to Ringo's—and after our show would go on to the pre-Disney *Beauty and the Beast* TV series (1987–1990), Guillermo del Toro's *Hellboy* (2004), and eventually a blistering run as the big daddy on *Sons of Anarchy* from 2008 to 2014. I run into him occasionally. He's a lovely guy, but he has nothing nice to say about *The Ice Pirates*. He doesn't shrug it off; I think he actively regrets it. He says as much in his memoir. No matter, he was fun to be with.

The whole company was. We knew we weren't making deathless cinema. But we had our fingers crossed anyway.

Every action hero has to have a sidekick, even in science fiction. Han Solo had Chewbacca. Luke Skywalker had two of them; true, they were both AI, but each of them thought the other one was just there as backup. We had Michael D. Roberts, a seasoned, in fact acclaimed, sidekick to Robert Blake on the hit series *Baretta* (1975–1978). After our little show, he costarred on an unforgettable bad idea for NBC called *Manimal* (1983), where he served as sidekick to a shape-shifting crime fighter, sometimes man, sometimes ani— You get the picture. For us he played Bob's faithful friend and cohort, and, as Michael was Black and funny and Bob was White and sly, it brought back echoes of the original *I Spy* TV series, if they had gone into outer space, an idea that is still available for rebooting.

In addition to a sidekick, every science fiction fantasy requires a supreme commander, the titular head of the evil forces that the heroes must conquer. In a world that had already met Darth Vader and Ming the Merciless, we had to come up with something pretty good. And his name was John Carradine. Even if you haven't heard of him, you've seen him, and you have certainly heard of him.

He is the nepo-babydaddy of all time, father of Keith Carradine, David Carradine, and Robert Carradine, grandfather of Ever Carradine, and is there a Carradine I'm leaving out? He has been gone for a while but is impossible to avoid on Turner Classic Movies. We got him at the end of a career that was as old and as storied as Hollywood itself, and let me tell you, he was a presence, on camera and off. We only had him for a few days, and his movements were even more strategically choreographed than mine—and I was a head with no body—but he did not disappoint on any level. A complete pro with a war chest of stories, he spent his time with us laughing at the people being deferential to him. He knew something about almost every movie that had been shot on the legendary Stage 30, where we were shooting, sometimes in the water tank built for Esther Williams and right next door to where the yellow brick road led to the Emerald City. The thing was that big. It had a tank and a town.

The picture was just about cast, but there was one small but significant role that defied the casting process. It was an alien creature, a female, who was human from the neck down and frog from the neck up. That's right. Frog Lady, we called her, and she is still listed that way on Marcia Lewis's IMDb page. Marcia was my next-door neighbor in Laurel Canyon. When you have a house in the Hollywood Hills, you get to know your neighbors whether you want to or not, because there are earthquakes, floods, plagues, mudslides, coyotes, bobcats, people who are stoned and lost wandering up to your door asking if you've seen their cat or have any peyote in the cupboard. And there is the inevitable night when you fart and the lights go out. All over the canyon. The infrastructure is very tender up there, or at least it was in the '70s.

I don't remember what particular crisis of nature it was that caused me to meet Marcia. It may have been when our dogs fell in love during a nocturnal walk and could not be separated, so we struck up a conversation to pass the time. Marcia was a brilliant musical comedy actress who spent a long time on Broadway and on the road as Miss Hannigan, the alcoholic scold who hates the title character in *Annie*, and in the '90s would be the first Matron Mama Morton in the still-running revival of *Chicago*. She got a Tony nomination for

The sign wasn't referring to me, except of course it was.

that one. Somewhere in there she decided to do a nightclub act and I helped write it, with Tracy Keenan Wynn.

She came running over the morning of the big Laurel Canyon fire of 1979 and cried, "Help me save my show!" We loaded her costumes, props, and sheet music into her car and off she went. The house survived, but that seemed to be secondary.

Now then . . . how can I put this delicately . . . she looked like a frog. This alone is a reason for you to watch *The Ice Pirates*. I remember coming home one day after listening to all the screaming rejections we were getting from agents and managers along the lines of "How very *dare* you suggest this for my client?" and there was Marcia, looking very sporty behind the wheel of her convertible, and I said to myself, "Frog Lady, I have found you!"

I summoned up a lot of vodka and pitched it to her and she said she would love to meet the people who had come up with this and just how much makeup would she not need? The next day she tooled in and stunned everyone. I had to hand it to her, she did wear something green. But they fell in love with her anyway.

In the movie, she is a very voluptuous, flirty frog lady who has eyes on Bob Urich, and she drives, with webbed feet yet, a block-long convertible hovercraft in a chase scene. The only issue was the tongue. Marcia did not have a frog tongue. She confided that there were times, off camera, when she wished she'd had one, but that was the kind of thing late-night dog walkers share, especially on dirt roads to the sounds of good neighbor Frank Zappa tuning up. Props, makeup—it was way before CGI—and probably a few other departments came to the rescue.

There were many other fascinating people in the cast. We had two very distinguished Brits. Actually, Natalie Core was American, but you would swear she was born pouring tea into porcelain cups. Her character was Mary Poppins to Mary Crosby's princess. Off-screen, she was salty, but in a very Angela Lansbury way. Ian Abercrombie, a certified Anglo, went on to play Elaine's boss Mr. Pitt on *Seinfeld* and the voice of the future Emperor in the 2008 *Star Wars* animated series *The Clone Wars*. Ian was rotund, impish, jolly, and delightfully obscene when the moment called for it. He, and I, later spent some days on a soap opera called *Santa Barbara* that ran from 1984 to 1993. Ian actually spent sixty-six days on the thing playing Dame Judith Anderson's butler. She apparently was saltier than Angela Lansbury and not the least bit like the dragons she played. I did two episodes as a biker priest, which is one character that didn't make it into *The Ice Pirates*.

In March 1983 the carnival of characters that did make it began filming *The Ice Pirates*, and as I recall, the first epic moments we shot were the scenes where Bob Urich and Michael D. Roberts almost get castrated. Strong stuff, even for sci-fi fantasy, where it is a given that almost everything in the galaxy has no junk at all—except in the stories where they somehow mate with a human. That was not on the docket here. Here we were operating on the ancient Roman theory that the best household slaves were eunuchs, because they couldn't impregnate the rest of the help or, Juno forbid, the lady of the house.

In our galaxy, prospective slaves are castrated and lobotomized, a two-for-one special that will result in their complete lack of drive to do anything but what you tell them to do in the near term. Our heroes have been captured and are sent to a "redesigning" center, but in the nick of time, one of their cohorts finds them on the conveyor belt and frees them. And that was day one.

Though we had the immense Stage 30, it cost money to build futuristic sets, even dilapidated ones like ours, and locations around town proved to be less expensive. The site for the redesigning center was the very space-age campus of CalArts in Valencia at the north end of the San Fernando Valley, close enough to hear the screams from the rides at Six Flags Magic Mountain. These were matched by the screams from the background actors playing men about to become slaves.

CalArts was heavily endowed, you should pardon the expression, by Walt Disney, and a lot of the place still looks like Tomorrowland or the Jetsons' summer home. It was perfect for us. The students, all art and design majors, which usually means weird and wonderful and high (they may have discovered glue before any of us), flocked to the cast, thrilled to have sci-fi creatures of every stripe roaming the halls looking for restrooms and vending machines. It would have been a big day for selfies, but . . . 1983. And the students began fading away from the set as it became clear what the scene was about. I am duty bound to report that everything went smoothly, and every time Stewart said "Cut!" there was a laugh.

For subsequent location shooting, we repaired to the massive Los Angeles Theatre, a two-thousand-seat movie house in downtown L.A. on Broadway—or, as it was known in 1983, Skid Row. In its day,

Broadway had been a street of baroque, rococo movie palaces, the kind that were originally built for vaudeville and later became shrines of escapism, places where ordinary folk could dream they were in the movies they were seeing. The Los Angeles was among the most distinguished. It's still there, occasionally in use as a theater, more often as a location for show business stories that need an old-school theater setting. A 2015 revival of the legendary-for-reasons-you-don't-want-to-be-legendary-for musical adaptation of Stephen King's *Carrie* pulled out most of the front orchestra seats, moved in bleachers, and staged the show in the round, with the mammoth open stage behind it used for effects. This time, it was a critical success. In recent years, some theaters along Broadway have been restored as part of DTLA, as hip downtown L.A. is now called, but the Los Angeles isn't one of them, so it remains ideal for an old-school location.

In 1983, nothing in the neighborhood was hip, and the Los Angeles Theatre was a Mexican porn house. It's important to make that distinction, because the movies were in fact Mexican, all the signs in the theater were in Spanish, and the clientele that showed up and pounded on the doors, ruining a few takes, were all Latin and shouted colorful Spanish curses. As you might guess, the theater needed a little cleaning up and a little relighting, but once that was done, the lobby made for a sweet throne room for a wicked emperor like Weird Wendon.

There was a sweeping grand staircase, easily twice as high as the famous one on the *Titanic*, that led up to a perfect spot for a throne, from which one might stare down at the peasants and cry, "Off with their heads!" Except it was Wendon's head that was cut off—actually, kicked off. Michael D. Roberts did it, swinging on a rope across the entire length of the cavernous lobby. It was a great effect, not achieved without some hard time on my part.

I had to drive to a far corner of the Valley to the studio of makeup wizard Matthew Mungle to give him head. I mean, *my* head, so he could make several replicas. He is a much-acclaimed genius at this stuff and is still at it today, this having been one of his first gigs. He had to make a cast of my entire head. In fact, he had to make two, one that the camera would catch bouncing down the stairs and another in case the first one got damaged in retakes. So for several hours, it seemed, I sat in a barber's chair, my face covered entirely in clay or something like it, breathing through two straws in my nose, not moving. It was like an MRI without the entertaining blasts of bomb-dropping noise. Heigh-ho, the glamorous life.

Then some time was spent while the wigmasters took measurements and snipped locks to make sure the heads' hairpieces would match my actual hair, which was not going to be a wig, which meant it had to be the same length every day of shooting. Heigh-ho 2, the sequel.

The first scenes we shot were a lot of fun for Michael and Bob. Michael got to fly across the lobby on a rope a couple of times to free Bob, who was being held captive by a group of Amazons. They were all stuntwomen dressed up like a futuristic roller derby team, and in or out of costume, you wouldn't want to mess with any of them. They were my Praetorian Guard, so I got to joke with them a bit, but it was clear they had a carefully rehearsed routine they were going to have to execute probably in one take, because there was a degree of risk involved. They had to defend their prisoner, Bob, from flying Mike and somehow all wind up in a pile at the bottom of the staircase. This they did brilliantly, with Stunt Bob and Stunt Michael carried along with them. Then the two stunt guys left and Bob and Michael took their place, entwined in this nest of boobs and buns and not at all eager to leave. There may have been a dialogue flub or two, which meant more takes. But nobody abused the privilege. When the crowd cleared, we did some shots of my fake head bouncing down the stairs. (I observed this from the concession stand, behind some stale popcorn . . . or was I still on the throne?) We then moved to the ladies' room.

Like many old movie palaces, the restrooms were downstairs from the lobby and covered massive acreage, as they generally had to service a thousand people or more at the same time when the movie ended and everybody raced downstairs. The ladies' room, as was the fashion, had an enormous vestibule with fainting couches, for women who needed a rest from whatever was going on upstairs or from life in general, as well as little vanity tables and mirrors so a lady could adjust her makeup before going back up into the dark theater or, to be fair, the brilliantly sunny outdoors. Beyond the vestibule were the dozens of sinks and stalls for the rest of the restroom resting.

Absent the ladies and the little tables, the vestibule was a dimly lit catacomb perfect for growing mold, made to order for an emperor's jail cell, which was where Weird Wendon's head resided once they discovered it was not dead. Of course, it wasn't spooky enough for us, so we added shaft-like mood lighting and a hurricane of dry ice blown about by a wind machine, which meant we had to strategically say the dialogue in between coughs and sneezes. There were a few hours of this until we staggered into daylight, rubbing our eyes and hacking up the catering.

Other locations provided their own hazards. Frog Lady had to power her desert hovercraft across a lunar landscape outside Palm Springs, fighting whipping wind, burning sand, and her diaphanous frog drag that kept lashing her cheeks. And there was the Space Herpe. It was like a motorized Slinky covered in goo. There was a radio transmitter so it could be controlled, but now and again it had its own agenda. No matter where we were, it would accidentally fall off things, attach itself to your leg like a young dog, or simply wheeze and die. All in all, it was a fairly festive shoot with a fun, anything-goes sort of vibe—that was the movie we were making. But we had no idea if it would work.

Things were moving along reasonably well when the next interesting thing happened: John Foreman was fired. MGM had made him head of production on an interim basis, we all knew that, but we didn't expect the axe to fall so soon. Overnight, he moved from the spacious office in the Thalberg Building back to the charming adobe hut that new people on the lot frequently mistook for a Taco Bell. The new tenant in the big house was Frank Yablans, the marketing whiz from Paramount's heady early-'70s run who, after he left that studio, returned as the writer and producer of *Mommie Dearest* (1981), a project which holds pride of place in the bad idea hall of fame.

Not the *worst* idea—that would be the stage musical version of *Mommie Dearest* that I was approached to write years later, but Frank, who controlled the rights, passed away before he could make it happen.

Frank and John were adversaries of long standing. As I heard it, there had been a dustup, old-school Hollywood style, when John was in business with Paul Newman and Frank said something disparaging about Joanne Woodward and John hauled off and socked him. This I gather was never resolved, and the first thing Frank did when he arrived on the lot was to announce that we had to finish shooting *The Ice Pirates* in eight days.

We had a few weeks left on the schedule, much of it involving heavy machinery and special effects and, well, there was just no way we could wrap all that up in time. And Metro still had Bob under contract, so leaving the picture unfinished was not a good look and would not inspire other talent to want to work at the studio. Everybody paused and took a deep breath to figure out how we could work this. And by that I mean we went into a group panic.

Stewart came up with the novel idea of having the pirate ship enter a hitherto undetected time warp, during which a lot of things could happen in speeded-up action, and when the ship emerged, the end would be literally in sight. This cut a lot of expensive and time-consuming scenes and made it almost possible for us to wrap on time. A lot of stuff wouldn't make sense, but that would be no surprise in this picture—and, truthfully, don't a lot of science fiction favorites make no sense when you parse them? People keep making movies about dystopian futures, but nobody ever explains how they got there, short of a lot of deeply intoned mumbo jumbo in a prologue. We did not feel unsafe in our time warp.

On the last night of the last day of shooting, after all the cuts that we could make had been made, we were sitting outside next to Stage 30. It was a balmy evening, there was a moon, we had just finished lunch, things that no longer would be needed were being crated and labeled, I was joking with Mary Crosby about what had happened on *Dallas* since she left, and the lights went out. All over the lot and all over Culver City. Just when I thought this picture had no more interesting things to offer.

Emergency generators coughed into life. A few dim emergency lights flickered on in dark corners, but otherwise it was pitch black. Soon there were sirens. We just sat there with weird, WTF expressions. Well, if you could see them. There were no smartphones to consult; it was as yet an app-free world. I think we all thought this was a glitch and everything would spring back to life in a moment. I mean, it wasn't a natural disaster and we hadn't heard an explosion. So we waited.

We also figured that those in charge would presumably have the situation in hand. A frail reed at best, but what else do you do in the dark? Run and sprain your ankle in a pothole? We were safer out here than in cavernous Stage 30, world's largest booby trap. It sported a million ways to kill yourself even with all the lights hot. So we waited. People came, people went, it got no brighter. It looked like it would either be a very short night or a very long one.

After a while, when we were on the cusp of group singing breaking out, John Foreman came by. He said the city would have power restored by morning, which of course would be too late for us. He hadn't bothered calling Frank Yablans, because he knew he would not be able to endure the howling laughter from the other end of the line. So he called Kirk Kerkorian, the fabled investor who actually owned the studio. He told him that we had a couple more setups ready to go to wrap the picture, but if we didn't get them, we didn't have a movie. With all the cuts, these small scenes were crucial to the story. The boss gave us one more day. We felt our way to our trailers and used flashlights to get out of our costumes and into our cars.

Dawn broke on a powered-up Culver City, and we finished the masterpiece with no further ado. There were more cuts and threats and double-dealings during postproduction, but I was on to the next bad idea. Nevertheless, interesting things kept happening. One year later, the picture was released. And John Foreman called Monday morning to tell me we had "a half-assed hit."

We went on to do reasonable business. John Huston was suitably impressed with his daughter's performance as an Amazon and cast her in his project with John Foreman, *Prizzi's Honor* (1985). She was terrific in that, and a year later won the Academy Award for Best Supporting Actress. Cable channels began showing Anjelica Huston movies, at a time when there were three: the medieval romance, *Prizzi's Honor*, and . . . *The Ice Pirates*. Media mogul Ted Turner developed a curious fascination with the movie and showed it endlessly on all of his channels. A few years later, I ran into a guy from the crew, a carpenter, who asked me if I had seen Mel Brooks's *Spaceballs* (1987) and if I had noticed parts of our spaceship in the movie. It had shot on Stage 30.

It's been forty years since we started the adventure, but thanks to the internet, *The Ice Pirates* will not die. Anjelica tells me that younger interviewers start off their shows by asking about it. "What do I have to do to get them to stop?" she wails in mock distress. As far as I am concerned, it is one of my triumphs for one reason and one reason alone: Weird Wendon made the poster.

5

Can't Stop the Music (1980)

Or, at Least Disco Was Already Dead

Nice as it would be to say that *The Ice Pirates* was the only bad idea for a movie that I was involved in, that's not the truth. There was an arguably worse idea with which I spent some time, and while it has not gone into the anals (and that's not a misspelling) of time, it's right up there. Real close. Maybe a few podcasts away. It was originally titled *Discoland: Where the Music Never Stops*. Can you guess what it was released as? OK, you get an extra juice box at recess.

I was actually physically present when the bad idea for *Can't Stop the Music* was hatched. It was in the backseat of a limo. Not as salacious as it sounds. The groundwork for the bad idea was laid earlier in the evening, when a group of Hollywood types piled into a black car to go to a TV taping. The limo belonged to Allan Carr, whose name will come up again in chapter 10 in relation to my initial skirmish with the Academy Awards in 1989. He was a very gay, very flamboyant, frequently chemically altered boy showman—the teenaged

Mike Todd, he called himself, shortly after he passed forty.* Allan had parlayed the management of actress Ann-Margret into a major career for himself as a Hollywood personality, a shrewd marketer, and the producer of the highest-grossing musical movie of all time for quite some time, *Grease* (1978). He was also the darling of the Hollywood wives, those spouses of movie stars and power brokers, the ladies who lunch. As a host, he was emblematic of the '70s, mixing old-school Hollywood with rebel Hollywood, gay with straight, chic with outré. Fabulous parties, some of them at his Hilhaven Lodge manse, some staged to promote one project or another at venues as varied as a high school, a subway stop, a jail cell, an actual billboard on the Sunset Strip—pretty much anywhere he could pull permits.

On this particular night in the late '70s, Allan had invited me to go with him to see this very hot, iconically gay disco act called the Village People. You may have heard of them. They still tour, and their music is still played at ball games where iconically straight people stand up and spell out YMCA with their upper bodies. The VP were taping a segment of *Don Kirshner's Rock Concert*, a syndicated late-night TV concert show that you could find on the non-network channels on the weekend. Allan was desperate to see them live, but in a controlled situation, meaning any place where he didn't have to take too many steps to get to his seat.

On the way to the studio in Culver City, we made a stop to pick up Jacqueline Bisset and her current paramour, the French movie producer Victor Drai. Victor had made some very funny pictures in Paris and was in the process of making American versions of them. He

---

* Mike Todd was a producer most famous for being husband #3 of Elizabeth Taylor (the woman who, for my niece's benefit, was once the biggest movie star in the world). Todd was a sensational showman who almost single-handedly produced *Around the World in 80 Days* (1956), which he almost single-handedly engineered into a Best Picture Oscar winner. He died tragically in the crash of his private plane . . . the *Lucky Liz*.

eventually gave this up and became a hot restaurateur, starting with Drai's in West Hollywood and later the Vegas club of the same name.

Joining us all was Bronté Woodard, a witty Southern gay gentleman writer, actually pretty wild when he got going, who had penned a beautiful novel, *Meet Me at the Melba*, which Allan, in his serious moments, wanted to produce, even though it was on the other side of the bridge from his wheelhouse.

This merry band trouped down to the *Rock Concert* set. It being Disco Night, and disco meaning dancing, the soundstage had some seats around the edges, but the audience was mostly meant to dance as the Village People performed onstage. There was champagne, as well as BYO everything else.

As soon as we arrived, we were pounced upon by the man who had created the Village People, Jacques Morali, a one-man *gaieté parisienne* who wrote, produced, and, with his straight business partner Henri Belolo, managed the troupe. There were some other disco acts on the bill, and while the other guests stomped all over the floor, we repo'd to a greenroom, where Jacques got to catch us up on his life story.

A few years previous, Henri was managing Jacques's songwriting career, which so far included a bunch of tunes lip-synched by spectacular topless women at the notorious Crazy Horse cabaret in Paris. This got Jacques to New York, where he dove into the gay club scene. He saw a Latin guy dressed as an Indian—now we would say Native American, but he is forever enshrined in Village People lore as the Indian. He saw people dressed as bikers in leather, sailors, GIs, construction workers, cowboys, all dancing like mad. And he had a vision. He would take these iconic American types and give them a little gay fantasy spin—one could say "sprinkle fairy dust" on them, if that hasn't reverted to being something that only happens in *Peter Pan*. They were all macho, but they were all dancing in unison. One of the song titles he came up with was, yes, "Macho Man."

He put the group together, relying heavily on Victor Willis, the sailor—the straight sailor, to be more specific, and the only one in the group who was a *singer* singer, the others being swell performers who looked and moved great. Victor also wrote some of the songs with Henri.

At this point in the saga, the group hit the stage and we went back into the studio and started dancing. You can spot us in the episode—well, you can certainly spot Jackie; the camera kept finding her, and she wasn't even wearing a wet T-shirt.

On the way home, Allan began percolating. He loved Jacques's story and thought it would make a great movie, but instead of Henri Belolo, he needed to have a fabulous woman as his partner, but not his love interest. If not openly gay, Jacques would have to be . . . hmm . . . dorky, that's it. That would leave the door open for the fabulous woman to bring one of her hot boyfriends in to help finance the group. Jackie would of course be the fabulous woman. And we would find some . . . hmm . . . dorky comic actor to play Jacques. We were all entranced with the idea, but we had all had a lot of champagne and probably something else as a chaser.

The next day, Allan told me that Bronté and I were going to write the screenplay from his original story, and I of course said yes. Sailors, cowboys, bikers—it was like asking one of the Brady boys to host the Miss America pageant.

The following week, I had a very serious lunch with Jackie Bisset and Victor Drai. I mean, we had fun, because they are fun people (who each have gone on to couple with other fun people), but they asked real questions about the project, things they needed answered by someone other than Allan. Allan didn't entertain a lot of questions when he was high on something, and I'm not talking drugs. If he was, like Mel Brooks's creation Roger De Bris in *The Producers*, in the throes of a stroke . . . of genius, he was phoning it in from a different plane of reality.

It reminded me of an old Hollywood joke about a woman who goes to a gynecologist, and the doctor notes, with some surprise, that even though she is married, she is still a virgin. And the woman says, "I'm married to an agent. He just sits on the bed and tells me how wonderful it's going to be."

Jackie and Victor wanted to know exactly how wonderful the writers saw it. But who could say? There was the germ of something fun about it, especially with all that music. And the contrast between a classy European persona like Jackie's and the collection of Greenwich Village party people she would be dealing with, not to mention her best friend and business partner, could make for some tasty conflict. I don't think they were convinced, but I know they didn't want to burst Allan's balloon so soon. It took them a few weeks, and he called to tell me Jackie was out—but he had a better idea. Who would be the greatest contrast opposite the Village People?

Mother Teresa, but she didn't want to do a musical and she always demanded final cut, so the obvious choice was the woman Allan had made a movie star: *Grease*'s Olivia Newton-John. OK, perhaps not a movie star just yet. Perhaps never, because the films that followed did not establish her as a motion picture draw, but the astounding success of *Grease*, coupled with her spectacular recording career, made her a huge name in the '80s, into which we were careening at the moment. In *Grease*, she had effectively parodied Sandra Dee, who *was* a movie star in the '50s and '60s. In the Village People movie, she might have a chance to parody Doris Day. Hard to say, because after initially showing some interest, she pulled away and made *Xanadu* (1980), another bad idea. Bizarrely, I was not involved.

However, before she had made her intentions clear, Allan, Bronté, and I sat around thinking up things that would make the part more Olivia/Doris. We looked at *Lover Come Back* (1961), where Doris and Rock Hudson played characters right out of *Mad Men*, if you beveled off the edges. Doris was a frustrated ad executive, and we thought Olivia might be something like that, only she had to sing as well.

We had an actual great idea, a real one, to have her be so squeaky clean, yet sexy, in a safe way, that the dairy industry would make her the spokesperson for milk. She would then get the Village People into a commercial built around a song called "Milk Shake," which had absolutely nothing to do with the song called "Milkshake" you're thinking about. The number stayed in the picture long after Olivia left to strap on roller skates and cruise around the rink with Gene Kelly in *Xanadu*. At the moment, she still hadn't made her mind up, or had the courage to tell Allan, or maybe face him after somebody else told him, so we began Olivia-izing in earnest.

Allan decided that, like all the great writers, we needed to squirrel ourselves away somewhere free of distraction. But he had an ulterior motive.

When I met Allan ten years earlier, he was about to go into the hospital for the first gastric bypass I had ever heard of. He described it to me over a plate of ravioli, which I rapidly stopped eating. I have never been thin, but I have flirted with being in some sort of decent shape several times in my life. Allan had been morbidly obese since his teens. He carried a ton of weight on what was a very delicate, short frame. Once, after a typical lunch for the two of us at the time, he sprained his ankle merely by stepping off a curb. He had tried many conventional diets, but the gastric bypass turned out to be the first of many unconventional ones that he flirted with the rest of his life.

There was one where he had his jaw wired shut and sucked all his food through a straw. He then went to Rio for Carnival and, my dear, you can't have your jaw wired shut *there*. You may even need it widened.

My understanding was the gastric bypass was what was constructed when they removed several miles of intestine, which they were supposed to hook back up after you'd lost the desired amount of weight and had, hopefully, "reeducated your eating habit," which is what thin people seem to have no trouble doing, but the rest of us, good night and good luck. The procedure may have changed since then, but Allan had such a good time losing weight that he kept putting off getting hooked back up and developed a gallbladder disaster that required emergency surgery. At least that was how he described the whole thing to me from his hospital suite, which closely resembled the garden Katharine Hepburn kept in *Suddenly, Last Summer.*

His weight had more or less stabilized since the crisis, but there were periods of yo-yoing. Allan's solution for this was to go to Hong Kong and have the same suit made in several different sizes on the theory that people wouldn't notice the weight gain—or loss, for that matter—as long as he was wearing an outfit they'd seen him in before. He could have opened a Big & Short shop in his closet.

By the time he decided we needed to really hunker down on the script, he felt he was a little over the weight he wanted to be. So he rented a house in Durham, North Carolina, ground zero of America's favorite fat farms, and enrolled all three of us at the one run by Duke University. Bronté, also a porker, thought it was the best thing possible.

My friends James Coco and Doris Roberts, two wonderful comic actors, advised me that I would be better off at the fat farm in Durham *they* visited, but I was locked in to the other one. The notion of dueling fat farms reminded me of my childhood in Paterson, New Jersey, where your synagogue was so much better than that other synagogue, the one where you wouldn't go if they gave you a million dollars. So we all went, you to your church, me to mine.

Our place was known as the Rice House. This was because the diet was, get ready, one bowl of rice three times a day, nothing on it, plus a piece or two of fruit. You could drink all the unsweetened coffee you wanted, but who wanted to be awake to endure the hunger? We would be there for a month. February, the cruelest one. Doris and Jimmy were at Structure House, which allowed you more food. I never asked how much more, because I didn't want to murder anyone.

Bronté and I made a rendezvous at LAX to discover that Allan wasn't coming. His client, Nancy Walker, the brilliant musical comedy actress and singer famous for being Rhoda's mother on TV and even more famous as the paper-towel picker-upper lady in Bounty commercials, was branching out into directing and she had scored a sitcom pilot, which Allan felt he must oversee. We would be in constant touch by telephone and fax. OK.

When we landed in Raleigh, the guy behind the rental car counter eyeballed us and said, "Goin' to the Rice House, are we?" "How did you know?" I asked. He answered, "Y'all will need a bigger car." "I beg your pardon," I replied. He smiled and said, "Otherwise y'all will spill your urine sample."

Say what now?

He explained. The Rice House diet was based on two things, near as I could figure: starvation and no salt or sugar. Very important, the no salt part. Every week, you had to provide the clinicians with a urine sample, which they would measure for salt to see if you were cheating. Since it was almost impossible *not* to cheat and remain sane, people got busted all the time. That they were paying more than their mortgage to lose weight did not carry much weight.

He went on to tell us the names of a few fraternities on the Duke campus that would put their pledges on a salt-free diet—which, granted, is hazing, but of a low order—and then sell the urine samples to "the fatties," who would pick them up and take them to the Rice House to pass off as their own. The road from Fraternity Row to the Rice House is filled with potholes, our man said, and you are almost certain to spill your urine sample. So you will need a heavier car. OK.

We piled into a Pontiac that I am convinced had fought at the Battle of the Bulge and trundled our way to our rental house, which turned out to be a huge suburban ranch number with every convenience, except food. We never tried the frat gambit, because we both figured, hell, we're here, why not let Allan Carr pay us to lose weight? But the weekly urine sample pageant always featured nervous-looking fatties who we knew were recent customers of Sigma Alpha Piss.

We'd eat all our meals at the Rice House itself, which turned out to be a dead ringer for Scarlett O'Hara's plantation in *Gone with the Wind*. It had a sweeping staircase that led to a landing where, legend had it, comedian Buddy Hackett, driven crazy by the program, had ordered pizzas and flung slices down to the fatties in the foyer before brusquely being told he had eaten all the rice he was going to eat in this particular establishment.

Bronté and I were the thinnest people there by at least 150 pounds. It cost a fortune and you had to be a very hard case with a lot of cash to afford it. Today, with a reality show called *My 600-Lb. Life* on TV every day, these stories are commonplace, but at the time, it was shocking to meet people who were so heavy they had made themselves immobile. And how they survived on this regimen I will never understand. Science.

While there were only a few cases *that* size, we were surrounded by extremely large, bell-shaped individuals. When the meal bell rang and they converged on the entrance to the dining hall, I felt like Elizabeth Taylor in *Elephant Walk*, at the climax when the elephants are all chasing her around the grand staircase. I told this to Bronté. "Don't flatter yourself," he said.

Across town, Jimmy and Doris were having a much more civilized time of it. We went to movies with them—never out to eat. We all were toeing the line. But their diets were not quite so spartan. I would seethe with envy watching Doris crunch into a celery stick while we sat through a movie about George C. Scott trying to get his wayward daughter out of the porno business.

But there were other things that helped take my mind off food. We had this improbable script to get out, built around a true story we were constantly fictionalizing, and one that had to be jerry-rigged for old Village People songs and new ones written just for the film. Three times a day we piled into the Pontiac to get . . . oh, look, rice! But this time there's a pineapple chunk! There would be calls from Allan telling us about this fabulous party and that spectacular luncheon and this mind- (and everything-else-) blowing gathering of young wrestlers in his pool house. And then one day he called to say Olivia was out.

This came as a minor shock, because in our delirium, we couldn't imagine she wouldn't want to do this masterpiece. Or that she would leave us for another, similar work of eternal art. Both of which she ended up doing. Allan being Allan, he decided Olivia was the problem. We needed somebody with a bit more show biz flair. While he pondered who that might be, we proposed that some of that flair could be provided by a supporting character we had been tossing around in between stealing apple slices from lunch and eating them in the car before they went brown.

Since we had established that our leading lady was not merely an ad executive but also a performer, it made sense that she would need an agent who would tell her how wonderful everything was going to be, but who also had a sharp wit and high style. We modeled her on Kay Thompson in *Funny Face* (1957), along with equal parts Auntie Mame, Holly Golightly, Sue Mengers, and William Randolph Hearst.

She wound up being played in the movie by the inimitable Tammy Grimes, and her performance may be the only good idea in the movie. She has a sidekick, a long-suffering, man-crazy kook like the kind Nancy Walker played more than a few times. I had worked with Marilyn Sokol, a terrific singer-actress and one of the funniest humans ever, and watching her interact with Tammy still makes me laugh. These characters, very much Allan's sort of thing, kept him going as he initiated the hunt for the woman who would be the center of the show. It ended one day when he called, uttered one word, and hung up. The word was . . . Cher.

Cher didn't know about it, no one told her this thing existed, and Allan didn't want to do anything until we had a script. So we set about turning Olivia Newton-John into Cher, which I believe Allan had already done in the big closing number of *Grease*, but I wasn't going to mention it.

You have to remember that at this point in our shared cultural history, Cher was not an Academy Award–winning actress. She had been in three movies, two of them under the aegis of Sonny, none of them memorable. There was no question that Cher held whatever screen she was on, but the jury was still out on how far from Cher she could actually travel.

It was tantalizing to imagine Cher as a Madison Avenue creative, a freaky one who did not swim with the minnows. But Cher as we knew her would not be at all out of place with the Village People, and the initial contrast between them and her was our entire character arc. Olivia projected a wholesome image but had a subversive streak that caused her to get involved with the group in the first place. With Cher, the difference between the image and the subversion was pretty much invisible. Nevertheless, we had to find a way to make it work.

By that time, our thirty-day detention was up and we got on a plane and I ate the chicken Kiev and a butterscotch sundae, which I may have salted for cause, and immediately gained back the thirty pounds I had lost. Back in L.A. and buying belts of various waist sizes—Allan had rubbed off on me in a small way—Nancy Walker's pilot had not been picked up for a series, and Allan was once again free to concentrate on our picture. Nancy Walker was also free, so Allan decided she should direct that picture. Her first.

You might wonder why Allan was allowed to make these decisions. *Grease* is the word. He had sold his Village People idea to EMI, a British production entity that gave him virtual carte blanche to make the picture he wanted to make. If they challenged him, he would say, *I made the biggest-grossing movie musical of all time, one with heavy youth appeal. What have you guys done? Not that, we'll just pick up the check and get a cab, thanks. Carry on.*

Allan had a couple of other casting items to take care of while Cher read the script. There was an elegant banker who our leading lady had to romance into putting up the money to start the Village People. Allan thought it was perfect for the legendary Henry Fonda. Bronté and I simultaneously bowed our heads so as not to reveal the eye rolls. We knew this was a fool's errand, unless Henry Fonda really, really, really needed money, which apparently he didn't.

The part was ultimately played by Russell Nype. He was a musical comedy actor best remembered for spending a year on Broadway in the early '50s opposite Ethel Merman in *Call Me Madam*, the part Donald O'Connor played in the 1953 movie version. If you don't remember him, it's not his fault. No one remembers who played opposite Ethel Merman in anything. Ethel liked it that way. But it gives you some clue as to how the picture was going when the part written for Henry Fonda was being played by Russell Nype.

For the knockout boyfriend the Cher character would fall in love with, Allan would settle for nothing less than Superman. Chris Reeve, who had recently flown that role into movie stardom, got the full-court press. A nicer guy you never met—that was his real superpower—and he was not the least bit interested. He was frying much bigger fish.

But someone who had absolutely nobody beating down his door for movies *was* available, and Allan saw him as the casting coup of the century.

Remember Bruce Jenner?

He was inescapable at this point. The decathlon winner at the 1976 Montreal Olympics, America's hero, appearing on Wheaties boxes from sea to shining sea—who would not want to see a movie with Bruce Jenner? We drove out to his house in Malibu, soon to become ubiquitous on television screens . . . OK, it took about twenty-five more years before that happened, and you know it wasn't the biggest thing to happen to Bruce as time went on.

We arrived to discover him fully dressed—shorts and a T-shirt, otherwise known as Malibu formal—and full of questions. He hadn't read the script, or maybe he had started it, but he was famously dyslexic and it was time consuming and I confided in him that he was the only person who would ever find this script challenging.

He was an extremely kinetic individual. I don't think you get to be a decathlon champion without being that. So we told him everything that was in the script and he thought it would be fun to do, especially romping around with Cher, whom Allan may have hinted was committed. As Bruce was before we got down the driveway.

Anyhow, how could Cher say no? Of course, she did. No harm, no foul; she was looking for parts with meat on them, not parts where she was surrounded by meat. Next stop on the hit parade: Raquel Welch.

This was more like it, although Raquel was always a tough sell playing anything but Raquel. She had turned in a very fine comic performance as a dizzy countess in *The Four Musketeers* (1974), but her director, Richard Lester, had told me it was a lot of work. He was also juggling Faye Dunaway in that movie, and nobody envied him having two glamorous divas on his hands. Besides, I, at least, didn't see Rocky—Raquel's nickname for herself—as a Madison Avenue ad executive who also performs dance numbers.

Actually, I saw the dancing part. I had given her some lines for her Vegas act. In fact, I gave her lines for various appearances throughout her career, and she pulled them off very well. She was perennially underrated. The thing about Raquel was she instinctively felt that nobody was going to take her seriously (some of that owed to experience as well as instinct), so she came on very strong from the outset, causing people to pull back. I think she tempered that as she went on. Years later when I was writing the 1997 Tony Awards show, with Rosie O'Donnell hosting, Raquel was preparing to follow Julie Andrews into

Victor/Victoria on Broadway. There was another show on the main stem that season, a musical about 1930s dance marathons in Atlantic City called *Steel Pier*. My joke for Rosie: "Raquel Welch is going into *Victor/Victoria* next week and they are retitling the show *Steel Pair*."

Raquel came up to me after the broadcast and said, "Hey—was that a tit joke?" I said no, it was a balls joke. She laughed, shook her head, said you have no idea.

She politely passed on the Village People, and a lot of other things, because she was looking to change her career. She did a TV movie, *The Legend of Walks Far Woman*, in which she played a celebrated Native American character. Raquel's father was from Bolivia, but that probably wouldn't count if they were making the movie today. When it aired on NBC in 1982, she got some great reviews and the ratings were very good, and there was much buzz about her career going in a different direction, but that didn't seem to happen. She did go to Broadway, very successfully following Lauren Bacall in a musical, but that turned out to be a one-off, too.

Before Raquel got the script and had a chance to say no, Allan said we had to rewrite it again and fashion the role specifically for her. We had already done two drafts of the thing, and I pictured us auditioning the script for who knows how many actresses, with tailoring each time—it was telling that Allan never suggested offering it to Ann-Margret—so I told my agent I thought we were due some more money. He agreed. And Allan fired me.

It bothered me only because—who wants to get fired? I really wasn't anxious to keep going with something that [*see title of book*]. Since I had ten years of friendship with Allan, I thought he might have handled it more delicately, but he was the kind of person who loved you if you agreed with him but had to push you away if you offered any resistance.

A few weeks passed and he started calling me to chat, and of course the chats were always about the movie. Did I like Steve Guttenberg for the American Jacques Morali? I did; Steve is a very funny light comedian, and we weren't asking him to play gay because, queerly enough, he had no real sex life in the script. Too driven, that was our excuse.

The picture was coming together quickly, which was scary—not to me, but to the people doing it. I had already told my agents not to challenge the writing credit Allan proposed for himself and Bronté, because I didn't want my name on it, not even a pseudonym, as I was so convinced nothing would ever come of the movie but exactly what came of the movie.

Allan cast a lot of his Hollywood wives and boyhood crushes in it: Barbara Rush, June Havoc, Army Archerd's wife Selma. Army was the last of the old Hollywood columnists, and Allan unfailingly took care of the press. Eventually, the Olivia Newton-John role went to Valerie Perrine, a real actress, so great as Lenny Bruce's wife in Bob Fosse's *Lenny* (1974), and so much fun as Lex Luthor's girlfriend in the Superman movies. She gamely took on the Village People and everything else life threw at her.

A couple of weeks before shooting was to start in the real Greenwich Village, Allan called me fairly hysterical. His energy level was always 11 out of 10, but he seemed particularly distressed this time. The lead singer of the Village People had quit the picture.

This was Victor Willis, the straight one who cowrote the big tunes with Jacques. Early in the writing, he had wanted to make sure he was not lumped in with all the other guys and insisted that we give him a female love interest. We only gave each of the Village People a life outside the movie in the sketchiest terms, and I mean *sketchy* in the sense of not a full portrait. So it wasn't difficult to write in a love interest, and it was easy to cast Victor's real wife, Phylicia Ayers-Allen, who was my future Oscar colleague Debbie Allen's sister. Jacques and Victor had recorded an album of disco songs with Phylicia, much coveted today if you can find it on eBay or in a bin at the Fourteenth

Street subway station, where I once found it behind one of my old comedy albums. It's the one with a gorgeous woman wearing a skirt made of bananas, in tribute to Josephine Baker.

Cut to: the movie is now in preproduction and Victor decides he's just too uncomfortable with the whole thing. He quits the movie, he quits the group, he quits doing everything except a few things he keeps on doing that have nothing to do with the movie. So Allan fires Phylicia. She eventually breaks up with Victor, marries the heart-throb sportscaster Ahmad Rashad, and becomes—Phylicia Rashad, Bill Cosby's wife on *The Cosby Show* and great lady of the Broadway stage. But I digress.

So there is a great rush to recast. Victor's part is quickly filled by Ray Simpson, brother of Valerie Simpson of the R&B duo Ashford & Simpson, and he's just fine. His character's love interest could be written out pretty quickly, but why ignore a chance to find the next Diana Ross and put her in there? The idea of casting *the* Diana Ross crosses Allan's mind, but it's quickly dismissed. He is racking his brain, trying to figure out who could possibly step up to this acting challenge, when he calls me in a panic.

But during the call, it occurs to him that last night's dinner guest might just be the answer: Altovise Gore, Mrs. Sammy Davis Jr. She had stepped away from Broadway, where she had danced in several shows, when she married Sammy ten years earlier. And she says just what Allan needs to hear. "Yes, I can."

I didn't hear much from Allan once the picture got started. I heard the usual things from people involved: this one didn't get along with that one, Nancy Walker had her hands full with a bunch of non-actors, things I expected to hear. I was surprised when after the picture wrapped, they brought in a crew of people who normally did music videos to shoot the elaborate YMCA number sans Nancy. Even if you loathe and detest the movie, that sequence stands alone and is pretty damn good.

I missed the spectacular premiere, which was accompanied by a party in a parking lot below a big billboard on Sunset Boulevard advertising the movie. The billboard had been tricked out with a shallow stage built along its length, onto which the cast climbed for pictures and to take bows. The structure remained for years, and in 1985 a computer chip company installed eight people in a proto-*Survivor* competition in which they had to live on the billboard until they couldn't stand it anymore, and the last one standing would win something that I hope was valuable. There were eight wall phones installed so each of them could have some contact with the outside world besides ducking the eggs that were thrown at them most nights as some sort of gang initiation. After a few weeks, it resembled a homeless encampment and the romance of the thing evaporated. It is now a permanent marquee for Netflix, which changes the message every few days to whatever new show they're plugging.

I went to see the movie at what is now the El Capitan Theatre on Hollywood Boulevard. Then it was called the Hollywood Paramount and was one of the last of the big movie palaces that hadn't been touched since the golden age. I sat in a sparse crowd with a group of friends who reveled in bad movies. We called ourselves Cinema Chien, French for dog, and we studiously picked what we knew would be the worst thing opening each weekend to watch from the balcony with popcorn and other substances. The picture did not disappoint.

The New Yorkers in the bunch noticed everything in the scenes shot in Greenwich Village, including local street characters they hadn't seen since they had moved west, and they cheered them on. The YMCA number got stunned silence as we looked at each other and said, WTF, that was good! The only lines I recognized from our scripts were in the Tammy Grimes and Marilyn Sokol dialogue, which actually got laughs from the real audience downstairs, such as it was.

Of course, the movie was a huge bomb. It wasn't all the movie's fault; it might have worked, but it was a year late. Disco Demolition

Night had already occurred in Chicago, when a radio station blew up a pile of disco records at home plate. The music business had moved on. From being the rage, disco was now the scorn. Except in Australia. There the picture hit at the peak of the disco craze and it actually did all right.

The Village People never went away—in fact, I wrote an album of songs for them with the real Jacques Morali. And I worked again with Allan Carr. And then the internet happened.

The wonderful thing about the internet is that failure is never forgotten, it's just a keystroke away. So the legend and the lore live on. Bronté left us just before the movie premiered, an early victim of the AIDS epidemic. Almost forty years later, I got to do a commentary on the celebratory DVD of the movie. What we were celebrating was never made clear. All I can tell you is . . . it takes a village, people.

6

Platinum (1978)

Or, at Least a Chandelier Didn't Fall and a Helicopter Didn't Crash

Bad ideas can occur everywhere, not just in movies, on television, and in plus-size roller derbies. The Edsel, for example, had nothing to do with any of the above. Twenty years later, my luminous Broadway musical flop *Platinum* didn't even last as many seasons as Ford Motor's memorable "cunt with headlights" (observed Martha Raye,* looking at the Edsel for the first time at a Miami car dealership, overheard by many, including a certain eleven-year-old).

Platinum actually started as an *interesting* idea that evolved into a bad one. A great Hollywood musical star of the '40s is now going out of her glamorous mind playing Mame and Dolly in summer stock ("One night I started playing Mame in the *middle* of *Hello, Dolly!*"). During a moment off the road, she is convinced by a sharp, young,

---

* Martha Raye was a very boisterous comedienne-singer who went from stage to movies to TV, eventually winding up as the spokesperson for a dental glue. She enjoyed taking her teeth out onstage to prove she was a customer as well as a spokesperson. She was a big star and big personality in her decades-long day.

gay, with-it mover and shaker to go into a recording studio and do an album of her hits . . . disco style. Yes, this is where Ethel Merman got the idea.

Also recording there is Alice Cooper, or a risible facsimile. He's a rock star who's turning thirty and feels the heat of the younger punk rockers creeping up on him. He is a huge fan of the movie star, has seen all her movies on TV and has no doubt had intimate moments with her image deep in the night. He's even bought her former mansion, because that's what rock stars do. Like her, he is world weary, but over the course of their weeks in the studio, they form a bond that becomes a relationship. It invigorates both of them and they realize that . . . it's never too late, you just gotta keep on keepin' on, the sun'll come out tomorrow—oh, sorry, wrong show. They also realize that there really is no place for them as a couple, they have gotten what they needed from each other, and their worlds can never be reconciled. So they part. Very adult.

The concept belonged to Will Holt, a folk singer and songwriter who at one point was very well known on the folk circuit as a performer with his wife, Dolly Jonah. If you can picture Elaine Stritch as a folk singer, you'll get Dolly. A very funny, very forceful, very inflammatory figure, she brooked no trout, as I was fond of saying. Will had written a big off-Broadway hit, *The Me Nobody Knows*, that premiered in 1970 and is still performed today. It's a bunch of kids singing the feelings that adults often don't realize kids have, and it was probably one of the first examples of a woke sensibility, a diverse cast shattering stereotypes. Will and his composing partner, Gary William Friedman, would try it again in the mid-'80s with senior citizens in a show called *Taking My Turn*.

In between came our show.

Will's idea was turned into a musical by a talented writer named Louis La Russo II, and it was staged in Buffalo, no less, directed by Tommy Tune, no less, with Alexis Smith as the Hollywood star, modeled in Will's mind after Rita Hayworth, who was still alive but beyond working at that point.

Alexis had been a star player at Warner Bros., playing opposite everybody from Humphrey Bogart to Errol Flynn to Jack Benny. When the movies stopped, she had taken to the theater with her husband, Craig Stevens, the star of TV's *Peter Gunn* (1958–1961). But she was not a musical star, until Hal Prince and Stephen Sondheim made her one in their classic succès d'estime, *Follies*. When it premiered on Broadway in 1971, the world discovered another Alexis Smith, one who had been lurking within all the time. She sang, she danced, she had gams and kicked them up like crazy. She also had a wry delivery and a sophisticated veneer, picked up during her years at Warner Bros. This masked a shy, insecure core that was probably the reason she hadn't become a bigger star. She didn't have that mania to be a star that almost all stars have. She didn't trust herself.

Alexis told me that she was discovered just like Lana Turner, at the soda counter of a drugstore. Only Lana's discovery happened four years earlier, near Hollywood High. Alexis was discovered in 1940 by a talent scout who saw her in a production at Los Angeles City College and followed her to the drugstore to discover her properly. And Lana was at MGM and Alexis was at Warners. But she liked to conflate the stories. I mean, they were as Hollywood as you get.

When *Follies* hit, Alexis was on the cover of magazines, all the talk shows, the rediscovery of the decade. She won the Tony that year, and they were raising glasses to her up and down both coasts. That was five years earlier. In the interim, she had not been able to capitalize on her great success on the main stem. There was a sad reworking of William Inge's play *Picnic* called *Summer Brave* in which she played the Rosalind Russell role people remember from the 1955 movie. Not glamorous at all, and a quick flop.

She'd gone glamorous in an all-star stage revival of *The Women*, but that petered out quickly, too. Her most notable film role was a notorious one in Jacqueline Susann's *Once Is Not Enough*, in which she played the lover of Melina Mercouri. I thought they made a swell pair, but more people heard about it than actually went to see it. So it was . . . interesting . . . that she was starring in this musical aimed for Broadway . . . in Buffalo.

The go-to person for this vehicle at that time would've been Lauren Bacall. She'd had a massive personal success on Broadway in the early '70s with *Applause* and was looking for another show, but I heard she didn't relish the idea of playing an older woman messing around with a younger man. Plus, she had already tackled issues of age in *Applause*. That *Platinum*'s original title was *Sunset* didn't help matters.

Will had chosen the title as a metaphor for careers ending, as well as a nod to the center of the West Coast recording business, the clubs along the Sunset Strip. But *Sunset*, coupled with the older woman / younger man plot, reminded people of *Sunset Blvd.* (1950), which, at the time, lived in fond memory as a nonmusical movie. In fact, Paramount, the principal investor in *Sunset*, also controlled the rights to *Sunset Blvd.*, and that was the reason our show had to change titles. Word was *Sunset Blvd.* was being worked up for Broadway by Hugh Wheeler and Stephen Sondheim as a vehicle for Angela Lansbury, but they did *Sweeney Todd* instead. And they never returned to *Sunset Blvd.* It wound up in Andrew Lloyd Webber's lap, and musical fans know the rest.

I was not involved when *Sunset* hit Buffalo. Will had conceived the show as a chamber musical, with the two leads being most of the story and a flashy young rocker chick modeled on Joan Jett being part of a triangle that would liven things up. He also had a surrogate Will, a sweet folkie working as a studio hand, called Jamie. He represented the unspoiled, optimistic side of the industry, and Will and Gary gave him a lovely ballad. Louis La Russo, the book writer, was having a moment, after his play in which a singer modeled on Frank Sinatra returns to Jersey, *Lamppost Reunion*, garnered him a Tony nomination in 1976.

The first problem was that Paramount was not looking for a chamber musical. Their vision was of a big Broadway show that would marry contemporary pop music with the swing of the '40s. *Sunset* had a cast of a dozen, no dancing ensemble, very *intime*. Tommy Tune liked it that way, so when Paramount revealed their plans, he left. He was replaced by Joe Layton.

The new director then replaced everybody in the cast except Alexis and Lisa Mordente, the hot rocker chick. Lisa is the daughter of Tony Mordente and Chita Rivera, who met in the original company of *West Side Story*, and it is not difficult to see her resemblance to all three of those entities. Brash, full of fire, energy, and talent, and schooled from birth in all the theatrical arts, Lisa is a force.

Louis La Russo also called it quits before the renovation could begin, which left an opening for a new writer. I had gotten to know Joe when we worked on Bette Midler's *Clams on the Half Shell Revue* (1975), a huge Broadway concert smash.

Joe was a tall dancer, like Tommy, and that's what got him his first job on Broadway in 1953, dancing in the ensemble of *Wonderful Town*, where the boys all had to be taller than Rosalind Russell, who was something of a giant onstage. He went from dancer to choreographer to director-choreographer in the era when dance took over Broadway, culminating in 1975 with the biggest hit of them all, *A Chorus Line*, a show about dancers. Joe didn't do that one, but he staged a ton of shows, many of them flops that he displayed proudly on his wall. I asked him why and he replied, with a grin, "They were not flops. They were all ahead of their time."

Bette's show gave him the opportunity to display his full shelf of insane ideas. It opened with the overture from *Oklahoma!* The curtain then went up on the first act of *Show Boat*. People toted that barge, lifted that bale, and hauled in a giant clam from the Mississippi. They pried it open and Bette popped out, dressed in full Esther Williams bathing finery, to launch into an up-tempo version of "The Moon of Manakoora," ending in the wild poi-ball-twirling routine she had learned as a kid in Honolulu. ("It was tough being the only Jewish girl in a Samoan neighborhood.") This was all Joe, except the joke.

When Joe was firing on all cylinders, he was brilliant. But he was in the shop a lot, as will become clearer as we go on. Right up to the cruel end of his life, I worked with him on concert acts for Diana Ross, the Carpenters, Lionel Richie, Siegfried & Roy, and others, and with Bette. At this point, as *Sunset* transitioned to Broadway, Joe suggested Will and I collaborate on a new version with some more humor and—here it comes—a more youthful perspective. I had just crossed the border into thirty, so I still qualified.

It being the beginning of summer 1978, we hied ourselves up to Will's family getaway on Golden Pond—actually Long Lake in the hamlet of North Bridgton, Maine. His family had been summer people for decades, and he had spent a lot of his boyhood there. It was a beautiful old house with a mudroom and verandas all around and Dolly Jonah doing a hilarious impression of a country wife while their ten-year-old son Courtney made periodic appearances to show us what he had caught in the wild. The Holts all loved that they were Democrats in the Republican bastion of North Bridgton, so much so that Will decided to register to vote there.

I went with him to the town post office, where the crusty old postmistress—think later Katharine Hepburn—had to blow cobwebs off the Democratic register to crack it open and enter his name. ("I see what happened when you moved to New York, Will.")

To take the show a bit away from the relationship of older diva and younger stud, we added the character of an understated but unabash-edly gay record producer, manager, and impresario modeled loosely around Allan Carr, David Geffen, Clive Davis, and others. We called him Jeff Leff, the former Jeffrey Lefkowitz who liked the rhythmic de-Jewishness of his new name. This was not at all uncommon among my circle of folk. He was around to remind Alexis, now christened

Lila Halliday, that this was a very important thing she was doing, this record. Jeff had the same fantasy relationship with her in his childhood that our rock star, now dubbed Dan Danger, had, with perhaps less of the sexual dimension.

Joe also felt the whole show should take place in the recording studio, which he envisioned as a shape-shifting room tricked out to put the artist into whatever mood they needed to be in. He wanted all the ancillary characters to be part of that specific environment. And, from his Bette days, he wanted the Harlettes, Bette's attitudinal but generally joyous backup girls. ("I call them my backup girls because that's what I have to keep saying to them. Back up, girls! Back up!")

He even hired one of them on the spot, Robin Grean, the tasteful Upper East Side White one sandwiched between the two feisty downtown Black girls. (We had toyed with calling the group the Oreos, an idea that later showed up in Barbra Streisand's 1976 version of *A Star Is Born*.) For the other two, he called on *Soul Train* dancer Damita Jo Freeman, a complete firecracker, and Avery Sommers, a belter who later was seen to much better advantage in *Ain't Misbehavin'* and *The Best Little Whorehouse in Texas*.

Suitably armed with explosive talent, we headed to Hollywood for rehearsals. Paramount had given us a soundstage on their fabled lot, just inside the storied gate Norma Desmond had talked her way through in *Sunset Blvd.*, with a view of the Hollywood sign and the huge blue-sky cyclorama stretched over one side of the parking lot that had once been the tank where Charlton Heston parted the Red Sea for Cecil B. DeMille and God in *The Ten Commandments* (1956). Here we were, doing a musical about old Hollywood and new Hollywood in the center of it all. My head spun like Linda Blair's.

There were many things to see on the lot, but the only one I remember was the stage next door, where a new sitcom set in a taxi garage was shooting. Attached to that stage was the Paramount gym, where an unknown actor named Tony Danza would spar with his partner in a boxing ring. I wouldn't call it stalking—all I can tell you is I was not the only one taking coffee breaks over there.

We were fully cast except for two major roles, and that was because of Alexis, who had approval on everyone and who, I suspected, was nervous about anyone she viewed as a strong personality. She was a lovely woman and nobody's fool, but she didn't have the confidence of a Bette Davis, who famously asked for the strongest possible actors to play opposite her because she felt it made her work harder and, ultimately, look better. Some really good people auditioned to play opposite Alexis. Wings Hauser, a strong actor, was too strong. Also too short, but Alexis in heels was, well, here's Rosalind Russell's third appearance in this chapter.

Rick Springfield, who was insanely hot at the time, wanted to do it, and he even came to Joe's apartment for a coaching session with us. I mean, he *was* a rock star, and how many of those wanted to do Broadway? Alan Sues—OK, he didn't come in for Alexis's love interest, he came in to play Jeff Leff, but he scared her, even though his audition was terrific. She only knew him from his sketch comedy work on NBC's *Laugh-In* in the late '60s and early '70s, and she was afraid he would start doing that goofy, over-the-top *Laugh-In* stuff onstage. I began to understand why, to a certain extent, she *was* Lila Halliday.

We rehearsed for several weeks at Paramount, and it became clear that Joe was entranced with the idea of the shape-shifting recording studio, and while he put the entire show on its feet, he wasn't terribly engaged with the actors. Except Alexis, whose hand he held, navigating her through every step. And she was letter-perfect, elegant, and professional, even though as soon as she left the stage, she was a pile of nerves.

She seemed to take to Richard Cox, now cast as Dan Danger. Richard was a Mick Jaggerish figure who later terrorized the entire gay population of New York in William Friedkin's controversial *Cruising*

(1980). He was exactly what we needed. Among his other assets was the way he looked climbing out of the fully functional hot tub that was a part of the recording studio. He was nude, but backside only. "Well, there goes the family audience," said Marvin Krauss, our old-school general manager.

On the last day of rehearsal, we staged the traditional "gypsy run-through," which I guess is now called the "Romany run-through" or some other sobriquet that doesn't offend. It's the final undress or dress, depending on what shape the wardrobe department is in, before the show goes out of town or into previews, and it got its name because the producers invite all the performers in all the other shows in town to see it, especially the chorus kids, who call themselves gypsies, or did. It's the very first audience.

In Hollywood at the time, there were no other shows, so a lot of friends of the production came. It went passably well, but I felt it was obvious that Joe had not spent a lot of time directing the actors. At intermission, Neil Simon came over to me and asked, "Is there anybody in this show we're supposed to like?" Not a good sign. Alexis was icy (she warmed up later), and Richard was arrogant (he softened that). But when Neil Simon gives you a note, attention must be paid.

We knew the buzz would not be thrilling, but that was a wonderful reason to be in California, which, in those days before keyboard warfare, meant you might as well be on the moon. Nobody was racing to the bar at Sardi's to trash-talk us.

We, meanwhile, were debating whether to keep the name of the punk rock band that had replaced Dan Danger at the top of the charts: Flaming Snot. I wrote it and I thought it accurately reflected the punk mentality at least two years before Butthole Surfers surfaced. Marvin the general manager, who already hated the hot tub and the nudity, didn't like it, but our producers did. One of them was at least Marvin's age, Gladys Rackmil, who in later years became Gladys Nederlander. Through two different husbands, she was full-fledged

Hollywood and Broadway. We called her Gladdie, like the flowers
Dame Edna tossed to the crowd,* and she was on my side. So were
Fritz and Barry, our lead producers, Fritz Holt (no relation to Will)
and Barry Brown.

Fritz was Hal Prince's stage manager and worked with Joe and me
on Bette's *Clams* revue. A terrific drill sergeant with a great sense of
humor, Fritz got the job done. Barry, his partner in business and in
life, came from theatrical marketing and was the yin to Fritz's yang.
He and I are still great friends. Flaming Snot stayed in.

We moved on, to Philadelphia, for the first tryout, in what then was
still the Shubert Theatre. Philly was a classic tryout town in the days
when shows *went* out of town. It's much too expensive now. They'll
do previews for a month if they have to, with New York audiences
from the jump. Back then, Philly was where you did major tossing,
trimming, and reworking, because it was the first time a paying audience was seeing the show and you sometimes knew right away what
you had to change.

The first thing that went was the overture. Joe never liked the
idea of one, but he lost the battle until we actually heard it with a
full orchestra and realized that it undercut what was a novel, unusual,
and effective opening sequence that brought Alexis into the recording
studio with a number that had all the punch and glitz of an overture,
and put the audience right where they needed to be story-wise and
atmosphere-wise. So we cut the overture. Wise.

In Philadelphia in 1978, almost everyone in the audience had seen
every musical on Broadway before it got to Broadway. And they let
you know it. At intermission I was like a bear cruising salmon as they
swam upstream. There was a physical resemblance, too, but never

---

* Dame Edna Everage, housewife superstar, later megastar, even later gigastar, was the
alter ego of Barry Humphries, an Australian actor of extraordinary intellect. I wrote
for the dame when she hit America and actually got her on *Hollywood Squares*. She
was a great favorite of the British royal family and punters everywhere.

mind. I was in and out of the crowds in the lobby, catching snatches of opinion. Not all of it was about the show. "Aruba is tired. We're doing this new place called Turkey Caca. Or Cacos, I forget." "I know it's a very loud orange, but it was on sale at Wanamaker's." "I think she's absolutely marvelous." "Alexis Smith?" "No, my new cleaning lady! She never sits down!" But a lot of it was about the show. "I don't get what she sees in him." "You shoulda been sitting on the side when he got out of the hot tub. I saw." "It's so improbable. A classy movie star hooking up with a sexy kid." "You never heard of Margaret Whiting? She married a porn star!" And a lot of this: "It's a long first act, but it looks beautiful."

They did like the set. It was wide open and full of screens that projected all sorts of scenes that changed the mood in the studio. And Joe kept things fluid. Alexis looked great in costumes designed for her by Bob Mackie, who is famous for making women look great.

And there was one element that caused audiences' jaws to drop. Among the things projected was a musical number from one of Lila Halliday's old movies. We had gone down to the *Queen Mary*, anchored forever in Long Beach Harbor, and filmed it in a day. Alexis, shot through a filter with lots of '40s makeup and wearing a snood, danced with our studio hands, now done up as sailors, one of them a handsome leading man. She looked fantastic, and at least one movie nerd grabbed me and asked if this was lost footage that we had somehow come across.

As for the second act, well, you never hear too much from a departing crowd that is dying for a cigarette (it *was* 1978) or a drink or a pillow. The show wasn't landing; it was almost there, but things hadn't jelled. Everyone else had an opinion, of course. It started with the Philadelphia critics, accustomed to writing a review that was more like a notes session, telling you what to fix because that's why you were in Philly. We read them over drinks and cheesecake at Frankie Bradley's, the Sardi's of the Delaware Valley.

The *Inquirer* thought Bob's red costume for Lisa Mordente made her look like a fire hydrant. That is how specific Philadelphia reviews are. The *Bulletin* thought Jamie's sweet, reflective, folky ballad was beautiful but brought things to a dead stop. And what did he have to do with the main story anyway? The faintly homophobic critic of another paper didn't care for Jeff Leff at all, although we only referred to his sexual orientation obliquely. He called him "one of the boys in the band," and said less of him would be a very good thing.

Alexis and Richard got off pretty well, although Richard's girlfriend, actress Rebecca De Mornay, slipped a note under my hotel room door with things she thought I should change that would help Richard's character bloom. They certainly would have made his line count bloom. Almost as much as what I tried to do with mine in *The Ice Pirates*.

The next day, we had a somber-ish meeting and decided that, much as we loved Jamie and the actor playing him, they both had to go. Will resisted at first, but saw he was outnumbered. We were guilty of not having developed that character enough. Whatever there was, it was all in that one song, which felt like it was from another show. And, of course, we were long. What musical in tryouts isn't long? I quote my late friend, mentor, and occasional collaborator, the great Larry Gelbart: "If Hitler is alive, I hope he's out of town with a musical." Philadelphia, here we came. And decamped after a couple of weeks for a lengthier tryout at the Kennedy Center.

On the train to Washington, DC, everybody was reading the hot new bestseller *Mommie Dearest*.* I mean everybody, generally with a dropped jaw. Except Alexis. I was sitting with her and commented that she seemed to be the only person on the train, if not the world, not reading that book. She thought for a moment and then told me

----

* If you don't know *Mommie Dearest*, the memoir of Joan Crawford's daughter Christina, I can't believe you're reading this book! I wrote the foreword to Ashley Hoff's book *With Love, Mommie Dearest*, about the memoir and the career-altering movie adaptation starring Faye Dunaway.

the following story, which is one of those things I could never forget, but just in case, I wrote it down the minute I got to the hotel.

"During the war, Craig and I had just gotten married and Warner Bros. sent us on a bond tour to raise money for the war effort. The first stop was Chicago. On the train with us were Joan Crawford and her husband at the time, an actor named Phillip Terry. We got to Chicago and we got off the train, and as we were walking down the platform, there was this commotion behind us. Joan got off the train and she was wearing a white linen suit topped off by a cherry red hat that matched her lipstick. The hat had a veil, and the veil had some fabric cherries sewn into it. It was quite a display. Craig said, "Well, she certainly came loaded for bear.""

"We went to the Ambassador Hotel, which is what you did on Warner Bros. money, and went upstairs to bathe and change and meet a few hours later for luncheon in the Pump Room with the press. I got out of the shower, and Craig told me Phillip had called and Joan wanted to see me. So I went up to their suite."

"Phillip said, 'She's in the bath, but she says it's all right.' So I went in. She was in the bath, all right, up to her neck in bubbles with a glass of something in her hand. And on her head was the hat. With the cherries."

"I said, 'Joan, are you aware that you are wearing your hat in the tub?' She looked at me, a bit out of focus, and said, very grandly, 'A great lady never bathes without her millinery.' I told her I'd be right back, and I went downstairs, and ever since then," and Alexis put her hand on mine and looked directly into my eyes, "I've believed anything anybody ever said about her."

She went on to say, "We all knew what was going on, but we assumed that it was the sort of thing people do when they drink so much they go into blackouts. There was a lot of that, you know. This was right around the time of *The Lost Weekend*—it was on everybody's mind. That and the war."

We arrived and got off the train and I was looking for hats with cherries up and down the platform.

The Kennedy Center is an imposing slab squatting on the Potomac. The Opera House, which you no doubt recognize from all those Kennedy Center awards shows where the dress circle is the closest thing to a royal box that you will see in these United States, was our venue. It's a great big house, and our great big set set the proper cavernous tone. You walk through flag-festooned marble halls to get to the men's room or anyplace else in the Kennedy Center, which makes theatergoing feel like an affair of state.

Audiences in Washington, at least back then, I found to be quieter than most. I think that is the nature of people who work in government and the diplomatic corps. They can't show too much emotion at anything. This holds true for a number of shows I've done in DC, and the Mark Twain Prize broadcasts. Audience members are very busy watching each other. Everybody looks like they know there are cameras on them, even when there aren't.

There are several theaters in the complex. The Eisenhower, named after a man who was more at home in theaters of war, features straight plays, and at the time we were trying out, the occupant was a tryout of a very serious piece called *Semmelweis*, about the doctor who discovered germs, to put it broadly, and campaigned for antiseptic procedures to be put in place. Every now and again I would walk into the lobby we shared and a door to the Eisenhower would open and I would hear an actor pleading, "Wash your hands, man, dammit, wash your hands!" Our entertainment looked lighter and lighter compared to that.

Our Philadelphia changes had helped, but the Washington critics didn't seem to notice. Judith Martin, better known as Miss Manners, the etiquette expert, wrote a review that was not in the least bit polite. I discovered that it wasn't just the Philadelphia critics who gave you notes. Once they know you are headed for Broadway, critics everywhere give you notes. The reviews should start with a disclaimer.

The problem with notes out of town is you only get so many hours to rehearse new stuff. You have all the time in the world to *write* new stuff, but actually putting it in the show is a nightmare. The legendary stories about things going in and out of shows like customers at a whorehouse must have happened before there were unions that regulate such unimportant matters as hours and schedules.

Real Broadway is tougher than summer theater, where it's not unusual to rehearse one show during the day and play another one at night, six days a week, maybe seven if the barn you're using as a theater is out of the way. If you're Broadway bound, you have to continue playing material that you know isn't working until you have the time to rehearse the new things. So we made surgical strikes every day, cutting here, adding there. The cast dreaded seeing us looming at the end of the hall. But it was fun afterward.

After the hand-washing ended in the Eisenhower across the hall, Deborah Kerr arrived to star in a revival of an old British comedy, and she and Alexis would hold court in the only place in the neighborhood that was open late, the restaurant at a hotel called, for real, the Inn Trigue. We were in Foggy Bottom, which is a part of town, not a sexual slur, near the State Department and, hence, a lotta intrigue.

Loads of people came down to see the show, my favorites being actress and TV host Arlene Francis and her husband, actor Martin Gabel, who hung out with us, if that is exactly the way to describe the hilarity of these most sophisticated people letting their hair down in a dark DC bar.

After what seemed like forever, we headed for the bright lights of Fifty-First Street and the rococo temple known as the Mark Hellinger Theatre. A temple no more, it's now the Times Square Church. The late singer-songwriter Peter Allen joked after his show *Legs Diamond*, not a hit, turned out to be the last show before the conversion, "It's fitting that it became a church. I spent most of the run on my knees . . . praying."

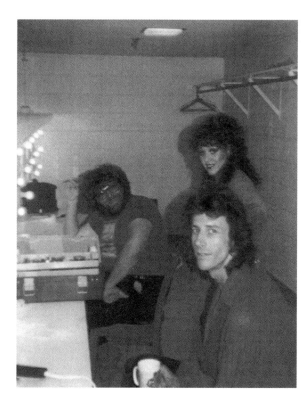

Lisa Mordente
and Richard Cox
invading my office
backstage.

The Hellinger had been built by Warner Bros. as a movie palace
to showcase their latest feature and maybe have a show onstage. When
they sold it, it became a legitimate theatrical venue, and a very large
one for Broadway. Shuttered during the war, it reopened, renamed
for the columnist and film producer Mark Hellinger, who had died
shortly before. Its most famous tenant by far was the original 1956
production of *My Fair Lady*, the *Hamilton* of its day. We came in after
Timbuktu!, a musical reworking of *Kismet*, with the action moving
from Arabia to Africa. Eartha Kitt was the previous occupant of the
star dressing room, and Alexis swore she found straw swept into a
corner, which either had been part of a costume or Eartha had been
keeping a camel in her closet.

And it was time for the first preview. There is a special kind of Broadway ghoul who shows up for the first preview. It's the kind of ghoul who can't afford a train ticket to New Haven or Philadelphia so he has to show up at the first preview so he can hotfoot it to Sardi's, fling himself at the bar, and begin bad-mouthing with a mouthful of peanuts. And the choice of pronoun here is completely arbitrary. But they were all in the house that night. Also there: the moneymen behind the show, Barry Diller (then head of Paramount, later creator of the Fox network) and Michael Eisner (then his number two, later the transformative CEO of Disney).

Augmenting the ghouls was the claque, those people who had become massive fans of Alexis during her run in *Follies* and were anxious to see her in another musical triumph. Claques are very vocal, and the screams and yelps of ecstasy that greeted her entrance might make you think she was a bigger star—and also might make you think the show was already a hit. I chose door number two, but it was a fool's errand. The show played all right, but there was a certain spark missing. We decided it was first-night jitters and whatever else we could blame it on, short of the show itself.

I went backstage but saw Barry and his not-yet wife Diane von Furstenberg* heading into Alexis's room, so I went to visit the rest of the cast. When I got back to Alexis, she was sitting in front of her mirror, looking a bit flummoxed. She looked up at me. "I called her Betsy," she said. Betsy von Furstenberg was a popular Broadway actress and probable distant relation by marriage to Diane. "First-night nerves," I said. "Send her a note." Alexis kept shaking her head, as if to say, *Maybe if I bought her a car.* The next night, another Paramount person came and stood in the back with me during the show. He said, "Barry liked it. Diane didn't care for it that much." Hey, everyone's entitled to an opinion.

---

* Diane von Furstenberg, once married to royalty then to media mogul Diller, was world-famous in her own right as the designer of the wrap dress.

I was mulling it after that performance when Michael Bennett, director and choreographer of *A Chorus Line*, walked up to me, full of energy, and grabbed my arm. "This show is extraordinary," he said. "I don't know that we can follow it." His latest show was *Ballroom*, also in previews. It opened shortly after we closed and became a much better-regarded flop than our show. But I was floating for days on his comment.

I was brought back to earth after the next preview by *Inherit the Wind*, *Auntie Mame*, and *Mame* playwright Jerome Lawrence, who I knew from the master class I took from him at Ohio State. His only comment to me was "Thanks for that cheap *Mame* joke." He was in town opening *First Monday in October*, a play about the fictional first female Supreme Court justice. "You can find me at the Majestic," he added, "with the hit show." It ran two months. But they did sell it

At Jerry Lawrence's townhouse, the little bit of heaven in Hell's Kitchen, 1969. He brought our eight-member master class to New York for a weekend of Broadway. Dead center on the couch is David Merrick, who *was* Broadway at the time, and looks like he's had enough of it.

to the movies. He was a great guy when he was the teacher and you were the student, but when you were in any way a competitor, which is how he must have seen me, you had to be dealt with.

The next day we all trouped off to *The Merv Griffin Show*. This was our first big promotional splash, and we were all pretty jacked. The show was syndicated to TV stations across the country, and its biggest market was New York, where it was a reliable igniting agent for ticket sales. It was right around the corner at what later became the Ed Sullivan Theater, where Colbert now rules.

The show was ninety minutes and Merv didn't do stand-up, so every moment was packed with guests. And what a roster he had. Ethel Merman. Opera singer Beverly Sills. And, of course, Bucky Dent, the Yankees shortstop who had been named MVP in the World Series and who did not seem to be a big fan of musicals or operas. But Merv sure was a big fan of his. Ethel, who became a real-life Lila Halliday with *The Ethel Merman Disco Album* (1979) after she saw our show, sang "There's No Business Like Show Business." You were expecting maybe "Eleanor Rigby"? Bubbles (Beverly Sills), also plugging a book, didn't sing. Richard, Lisa, and the three principal backup singers did a medley of their numbers, and Alexis, looking glorious and casual at the same time, did the talking to Merv.

We faked that it was opening night, knowing that was the scheduled airdate of the show, a few days away. It was a real New York moment, marrying Broadway, Hollywood, rock 'n' roll, sports, books—it was like a table at Elaine's—and we sold a few tickets off it. Merv's reputation was not unfounded.

A few nights after it aired, one of my mother's canasta cronies from Jersey and her friends came to the show. During intermission, I went down to their seats to say hello. A guy in the row behind them said, "You're the writer, yes?" I nodded. "Does it get any better?" he asked. "No," I said, managing a laugh. "You can leave now." He wasn't expecting that, nor the laugh it got from the ladies.

The next day was another troupe movement. We went to shoot the commercial. This was a newish thing at the time. Broadway was always mainly marketed through the press, this being the Paleozoic Era before internet and smartphones. *Pippin* broke the ice in 1972 and did so well with their hot, sexy commercial that other shows began jumping in.

At the time, the Henry Miller's Theatre, a lovely legit house, had spent some time as a porn cinema—this was Times Square in the '70s—and, after it was thoroughly trashed, was converted into a disco called Xenon. Xenon had fabulous projections and glamour and it was decided by the marketing people that the show would look much better there than on our actual stage, so they shot a commercial at the club that looked like a movie, only not a very expensive movie, but it was a very expensive commercial. Paramount had to put in extra money for this, as commercials were not yet standard operating procedure. If we sold tickets off of this sixty seconds of nonstop thumping action, I'll bet people who came to see the show were a little deflated when they encountered the real thing.

There was nothing left to do with the show but open it. The New York newspapers had been on strike all through our rehearsal and out-of-town tryouts, so some shows had opened in the dark, which is one reason we did the commercial. Our mazel, we would be the first show the critics would see after their self-imposed hiatus. I could hear the knives sharpening from the East Side to the West Side.

I don't remember the opening night being that glamorous. There wasn't a red carpet to walk or a step-and-repeat to pose in front of, which these days are de rigueur for the opening of a pet supply store. The afterparty was at Roseland, which had the advantage of being around the corner—it was a brisk November evening. The famous dance palace had seen much better days, but it served as a party space almost in keeping with the setting of the show, somewhere between rock, disco, swing, and Broadway.

Before the afterparty was the show itself. I stood in the back, near but apart from Barry Diller, in a firing line of my colleagues. Alexis entered to a fine ovation and launched into the opening number . . . which was flawless . . . and stopped the show. And it never started again.

I will not defend my contribution as particularly inspired, though there were laughs. But what had been clear to me from the early days at Paramount stared out at me from the stage: Joe had staged the show, but he hadn't directed it. Relationships between the characters were vague, and they were lost in the vastness of the set with all its technical wonders. I felt the audience silently slipping away from us. One by one, we looked at each other and knew something was terribly wrong, something we should have fixed three cities ago. There was a ripple of interest when Richard Cox emerged from the jacuzzi. And there was something none of us had ever addressed. The musical score was right down the middle, rock 'n' roll and Broadway. People who liked the rock 'n' roll hated the Broadway, and vice versa. And neither was terribly strong.

Of course, the script could have been better. My favorite review was the one that said things only got started at the end of the first act when the writers decided to give us a real scene. That was the scene where Lila and Dan realize they are falling for each other, and I had written a lot of it. No surprise that was my favorite review.

Richard Eder, who came from running the *New York Times* bureau in Paris to serve as a theater critic for a year, including downtime for the strike, was particularly vicious. OK, maybe not particularly, but it was in the *Times*. He seemed to resent having to get back to work just to review this show. There were some positive notices, but all of them had some variation on the platinum pun—the *New Yorker* headline was TIN. I expected that, but it stopped being fun watching how it played out.

In the days following the opening, there were many meetings about what to do. Traditionally, when a show opens to less-than-ecstatic reviews, the marketing people either go into full swing or they tell the producers not to throw good money after bad, just close the show, cut your losses, and ease on down the road. This was the prevailing attitude on our production, for a couple of reasons.

Sometimes a show can get enough asses in seats just through the advance sales. But Alexis turned out not to be Lauren Bacall. While the claque all showed up, there was not a groundswell of interest in her return to musical theater. We feared this, which is why we were hoping reviews would save us. The other way to go was against the wind, spend money on marketing. But there was no money to spend. The show had cost the unseemly sum of $1.5 million to bring in, which in those days was about as high as an elephant's eye.

Paramount was in for a lot of that; the Nederlanders (owners of the Hellinger), the Kennedy Center, and the Shuberts (Philadelphia) also had significant chunks. They weren't going to up their ante. Paramount had the movie rights, so we couldn't go to another studio and use them as an inducement. Will and Gary had a deal with Warners to record the album, so we couldn't go to another record label. We would have to approach individuals and ask them to have faith that the word of mouth engendered by the marketing spend would overcome the lukewarm critical reception. Turns out we were of the wrong faith.

I went back to Hollywood, where I might not hear the axe fall quite as loudly. The show scared me away from Broadway and back to television and live concert work, where I was a success. I subsequently worked with Joe on a lot of things that did not require a book. As Adam Gopnik once pointed out in the *New Yorker*, *the* book is what theater people call the libretto. *A* book is what they call revenge. This chapter is not that.

When I did come back to New York on some other project a few months later, I went to Joe Allen's theater restaurant. Joe decorated the walls of his place with posters of legendary flops, not unlike Joe

Layton's office. I looked around warily but couldn't find *Platinum*. When Allen stopped by, I told him I was grateful there was no poster. He asked me how long the show ran. Thirty-three performances. He said, "What, are you kidding? You were a smash! You gotta close in New Haven to get on this wall!"

Turns out it's not just hard to get famous, it's hard to get infamous, too.

7

Three/Comedy Tonight (1994)

Or, at Least This Didn't Make Joe Allen's Wall, Either

I don't want you to think *Platinum* was the only bad idea I had on Broadway. Please. That one ran thirty-three performances (and twelve previews). I had one that ran nine performances (and five previews), and to add heartbreak to the mix, it closed on Christmas Day 1994. If the ghost of Christmas future had told me a year before to steer clear, I might have listened, but I was busy lighting Hanukkah candles.

There was no Scrooge involved with the show; in fact, the prime mover behind it was an extravagantly generous producer named Alexander H. Cohen. Alex the Great, we called him. He and David Merrick were the Barnum and Bailey of midcentury Broadway, pulling outrageous promotional stunts for their shows but producing interesting shows withal, even the flops.

Alex had been inspired by a show called *Catskills on Broadway* (1991–1993), in which three or four comics who had done time on the borscht circuit brought their acts to a Broadway house and ran for over a year on what was left of the traditional Jewish New York audience and the Gentile friends they had prodded into seeing the show. Alex's idea was to go into the same theater with three performers doing a show that would have something for a different audience. It would be very New York and very smart, but not ethnic.

His stars were Dorothy Loudon, a sophisticated musical actress and comedienne, Mort Sahl, the razor-sharp political comedian, and Michael Davis, a handsome, bright, charming leading man who juggled for a living, but his act was clever and had a few tricks in it worthy of Cirque du Soleil. Alex called the show *Three*.

He got John Kander and Fred Ebb to write an opening number by that number. It was all about how wonderful threesomes are, without explicitly saying that, and it was performed by all three stars, who would then be seen in half-hour doses of their own material. You may wonder where I came in. Stamford, Connecticut. That toddlin' town.

I got a call from Alex asking me to come there. I'd met him a few years before when I cowrote my first Oscar show with his wife, Hildy Parks, a whip-smart individual who had written all the great Tony Awards shows that had put Alex on the television map. He told me he was having a bit of a problem with Dorothy Loudon. I'd worked with her, too, and I understood what that might be. Dorothy had been a cabaret darling in the '60s, and after many flops and much TV, in 1977 she got the role of a lifetime, the original Miss Hannigan in *Annie*. Suddenly, she was a star, but after a few more things didn't happen, she was only a star to a devoted coterie. A success in the Broadway production of *Noises Off* in the early '80s didn't lead to anything big, and she began to become what could delicately be called a troubled collaborator. Could I come in and write her some new stuff?

It seemed like a bad idea at the time, but I was a big fan and we'd had fun previously. So hello, Stamford. The show was breaking in there and rehearsals were going fine when Michael and Mort worked, because they knew what they were doing. Dorothy was very much at sea. She had been married for years to an extremely talented pianist and arranger named Norman Paris, who had put an act together for her decades ago. Tragically, he died a few months into the run of *Annie*, at the height of Dorothy's success, and she never really got over it.

She also never got over the act he had written, either. She was still doing it. A piano, a feather boa, some witty but dated material, and a performing attack that had worked in small clubs but didn't translate to the theater stage. She hadn't worked up anything that needed to *be* staged, really—it was all as if she were working in a tiny spotlight at Le Ruban Bleu, or some chic boîte of the ancien régime. Part of her thought it would all work. But part of her knew it wouldn't.

And that was where she spent most of her time mentally, in that chasm between those two thoughts. Changing anything was a terrifying prospect. But so was bombing. So she was interested in new material, but afraid of it because it was new. A strong actress, she had no character to play. Or, rather, she did have one—the Dorothy Loudon cabaret character that she trucked out for awards shows and benefits was wonderfully funny—but all the material for it was site specific. She needed new stuff and she needed it yesterday. But she wasn't going to learn any of it, because she was in a panic that immobilized her.

Alex had put her in front, right after the opening number, because she was the theater star, but really because he was afraid to make her follow the two pros who had it together. It was too late to do anything new musically, so I tried to get her to talk about her career in between the numbers, anything that could connect the songs and give her a throughline, but the panic covered that, too.

The first preview was excruciating. The opening number was terrific, then she made a quick costume change and came out and launched into pretty much the old Persian Room act, which not too many suburbanites in the crowd understood, as they did not live in Manhattan and did not know what a Zabar's was.

When she came offstage, I went into the wings and said, "Tough crowd," and she said, "I thought they were sweet." I realized I was confronted with someone who maybe had a slightly altered sense of reality. "Now that we've broken the ice, it'll be much better," she said, and I didn't hear the rest because of the roar of laughter that was coming from the people watching Michael Davis juggle chainsaws or something.

The next day she developed a flu and didn't think she could perform. Alex, who was nothing but solicitous at first, said he would take care of it, and after an explanation to the audience, he had Michael and Mort do more time that night. She wasn't well enough to work with me the next day, so I wrote some stuff and slipped it under her door, and she called the next morning and said she liked it and was trying to learn it.

The next performance was more uncertain than the opening. She got through it, but she was confused and a little discombobulated. The flu came back. And Alex went into action. That night, he explained Dorothy was unwell and the audience should all enjoy a new comedienne he had found. And Joy Behar took the stage.

I had heard great things about her from Kaye Ballard, a comedic Broadway star many remember from her TV series *The Mothers-in-Law* (1967–1969). Kaye had done a show with Joy and was a perceptive audience. And she was right. Joy had them from the moment she took one of the day's biggest stories and said, "Salman Rushdie is getting married. He has been in hiding for two years. I am standing right here and I can't get a date."

It was the start of something big. By the next morning, Alex had signed her as Dorothy's standby and Joy was living in the hotel with the rest of us.

Dorothy rallied the next night. She learned some of the new material, she performed it with some degree of authority, she got some laughs, and, for a moment, she was on even keel. I had a drink with

Alvin Colt, the Broadway brahmin who had designed her dresses, and I said things were looking up, and he cocked his head with a look that seemed to say . . . *maybe.*

I have to point out that when I actually sat down and worked with Dorothy, we had a lot of laughs. But the moment she needed to commit to something, the self-doubt would take over. It was very frustrating, especially for someone who had seen her at her best and knew how spectacular she could be.

The next day Alex went up to her suite and told her he was putting Joy on the show permanently, alongside the original trio. Instead of being called *Three*, the show was now going to be called *Comedy Tonight*, and if someone thought it was a Sondheim revue, so much the better. Kander and Ebb's number was scrapped—I was hoping it might show up in their 2023 Broadway production *New York, New York*, but no such luck—and the gorgeous set with representations of the numeral 3 all over it went the way of a failed troika, too. Now we were 4.

The good news about this was that Dorothy didn't have to do as much time, and she was not displeased. She still opened the show, and Mort still closed it. They were now the two adults and Joy and Michael were the kids who got all the big laughs. Armed with a structure that seemed to work, we headed to New York and into the Lunt-Fontanne Theatre.

Not even Dorothy could call the preview audiences sweet. They gave her a roaring ovation when she entered, which made me think she was going to rise to the occasion and really deliver, but she was all over the place. Some things that had worked in Stamford suddenly didn't work, some things that had been tossed out reappeared, and yet there were moments of brilliance—an offhand remark, a bit of body language. It was very uneven, and I was hearing some material that had come from some unknown source(s), for which I was blamed by some critics. My billing was "Special material for Ms. Loudon contributed by," so I suppose I was asking for it. I didn't think it would matter in the long run, because it was clear this was not going to be a long run. Joy scored, Michael scored, and Mort got an oddly lukewarm reaction from a theater crowd that probably hadn't loved him so much to begin with. He always was a polarizing force.

We were surrounded by Christmas that one week we ran, but nobody was in a holiday mood, and to tell you how bad things were, the week between Christmas and New Year's is usually the biggest week of the year, and we didn't even have much of an advance for *that*. Things tend to plummet after January 1, and Alex made the wise decision to cut his losses. Everybody but Dorothy had an easy time picking up gigs in resort cities to fill their winter calendars. She went back to her apartment.

A few years later, Clint Eastwood, who it may surprise you to know is a fan of cabaret singers, lured her out for a funny role in his film adaptation *Midnight in the Garden of Good and Evil* (1997), but her live performance days seemed to be over. She didn't get out much, which spared her seeing the poster for *Comedy Tonight* enshrined on Joe Allen's wall of shame. It may have had a brief run even there, so she probably would have missed it anyway. Now that's saying something.

8

The Look of the Year (1988)

Or, at Least the Sushi Was Fresh

Humble brag. I am the EGOT of awards show writers. It is a very humble brag because I'm not the only one who has written the Emmys, Grammys, Oscars, and Tonys. There are probably more EGOT awards show writers than there are actual EGOT winners.

My favorite bad idea for an awards show was *The Look of the Year*, a modeling competition sponsored annually by the Elite modeling agency, and the only reason I did the 1988 show was that it took me to Japan. Well, you know it wasn't the anorexic teenage girls with threatening cheekbones. Wrong room.

And wrong Japan. We did the entire show at a Japanese beach resort called Atami, where drunken men in kimonos sprained their ankles on cobblestones going from pachinko parlor to pachinko parlor. There were brief glimpses of some of the other Japan from the windows of the bullet train as we streaked back and forth across the landscape for the occasional production meeting with our Japanese counterparts, who steadfastly refused to leave Tokyo.

From what I could gather from our tight-lipped liaison, Atami was kicking in some yen for the exposure the resort would get on American television, not to mention around the world, as Elite models were flying in from all over the globe for the competition. I flew in with Ashley Hamilton, whose father, *the* George Hamilton, was hosting the show.* Ashley later became an actor, too, but for me he was always the guy who taught me the cure for hiccups, which I will share in another book that will really sell.

In addition to George hosting and dozens of models flying in, our invasion force consisted of a panel of judges, including Stephanie Beacham, a warm yet caustic British actress starring on ABC's *Dynasty*, and magician David Copperfield, because there is no fashion without magic. There were also some judges from the rag trade who would tip the vote toward whomever they thought could really sell something by wearing it or smelling like it.

For entertainment between the parade of pulchritude, we had Louie Anderson before he became a serious actress (playing the mother on the FX series *Baskets*), and the Pointer Sisters—then Ruth, Anita, and June—who were at the height of their record-selling fame. They were great hits wherever they went in Japan, and not just because they had performed there before and were well known. Japan in 1988 was still a country where everybody seemed to dress like everybody else and Westerners, especially ones who wore loud colors or unusual styles, were viewed with wonder. They worshipped Michael Jackson. That was always the first question they asked: *Is Michael on the show?*

I had worked with the Pointers ten years earlier, when they were wearing their grandmother's old church clothes and making it a fashion

---

* George Hamilton: MGM's pretty boy of the late '50s–early '60s who became an adept light comedian and one-man embodiment of suave. He has a great sense of humor about himself.

statement. They would enter to their first hit, "Yes We Can Can," later used by Barack Obama as a campaign theme. There was a clothing rack upstage with a bunch of feather boas on it, and as they came on, each sister would grab a different boa and they would go into their opening number. Magic. Now they wore the most outré things they could find, and the shopkeepers on Omotesando, Tokyo's "street of teenagers," saw them coming.

Louie Anderson's luggage had gone missing, so we went into Tokyo to get him some show garb. We had no idea where to go, so Louie waltzed into the Imperial Hotel, a Frank Lloyd Wright–designed building that is still a landmark, to find a store. After a short conference, he came over to me and said, "I told the guy I was looking for a big and tall shop. He said, you need huge and monstrous. So I asked him where Godzilla gets his clothes."

I told him we should look for a synagogue and somebody there would have a garment guy in the family.

Louie's was not the oddest request I got on the trip. The Pointers were not big lovers of raw fish and asked where they could get some fried chicken. I did a little digging and discovered a Popeyes in the city of Odawara, which was conveniently the stop right before Atami on the bullet train. We took the train up, bought the birds, and took them back on the train, getting stink-eye stares from more than one bento-box diner.

The easiest of the strange requests came from George Hamilton, who quietly said to me one afternoon, "Do you happen to know anyone in this town with a tanning machine?" I thought for a moment. "I happen to know David Copperfield. He travels with one." "For an illusion that he does?" "You might say that."

David and I spent a lovely few hours watching George slowly roast as we gossiped about the finer points of maintaining a five o'clock shadow all over your body.

The show itself was, well, a beauty pageant. Mostly it was the girls, and there were a lot of them, strutting about in various outfits.

George got to ask the inane questions and have some light patter to amuse the models, and he put all of that over with aplomb, and the Pointer Sisters rocked. Louie Anderson was terrified that the Japanese audience wouldn't understand a thing he was saying, so we imported busloads of American military from bases around the country. They laughed at everything he said, but the rest of the crowd stared at him, probably wondering where he'd bought his outfit.

The highlight of the trip for me was an excursion with some of the gay members of the staff to Roppongi, the nightclub district of Tokyo, where we were specifically directed to one of the strangest places I've ever been.

Space for everything is at a premium in Japan, which I first noticed in my hotel room, very luxurious but clearly built for a tourist not as huge and monstrous as my own self. In Tokyo, every square inch is spoken for, and the six-story building we entered in Roppongi was no exception. There was a tiny elevator and we were told to go to the top, but the elevator would stop at every floor, because that's how it was programmed. The door would open on each floor to a different type of gay bar.

Floor 2 opened onto a sea of men and women in tuxedos with cigarette holders. A dress bar.

Floor 3 was cowboys and the occasional Native American samurai.

The fourth floor was leather and the hum of Harleys.

The fifth was military.

I thought, leave it to the Japanese to turn the Village People into a building.

The top floor was Speedos, bikinis, jock strap, and flip-flops, and I'm not talking about shoes.

We got back to Atami to witness a military chopper lifting off with our executive producer as the only passenger. He was being airlifted out because the Yakuza had made threats against his life. He had evidently made some deals with the local mafia to get some things vital to the production of the show and had to get out of Dodge because something had gone south, as my translator put it to me. I think he learned English watching *Gunsmoke*.

9

Charo (1976) and Henne (1991)

Or, at Least It Wasn't *The Love Boat* (or We Would Have Had Charo and Carol Channing in the Same Show)

Some bad ideas have been built around some very good people. It was a bad idea to build a sitcom around Charo.

First of all, you can't build anything around Charo, she will simply break out of it and be Charo. She is a force of nature, a natural-born showman, a sensitive classical flamenco guitarist—no, that's not a stray phrase from another page. She studied guitar under Andrés Segovia, which sounds like a joke she would make and then look at you and wonder why you are laughing. That is one of her favorite gambits, the *I'm so dumb I don't know what I'm saying* pose that dozens of women have used to get laughs. It still works, even though most of them are dumb like a fox, to use an expression as old as the gambit.

So: Charo. Big hair, big boobs, big hips, big sequins, big smile, and a catch phrase, "*Cuchi-cuchi!*" that means whatever she wants it to mean. Sex, dancing, feeling good, sneezing, she uses it interchangeably.

The biggest thing about Charo is her brain, topped only by her good nature.

She started as the last Mrs. Xavier Cugat. Coogie, as everybody but Charo called him, who discovered her in Madrid, was a very successful Latin bandleader who had a series of glamorous singing wives, most notably Abbe Lane (full disclosure: I worked with Abbe, too, which was a *good* idea). By the time he brought Charo to the States and married her (to get her into the country, as she tells it) he was in his midsixties and she was maybe twenty, no one really knows, but more about that later.

At this point, the mid-'60s, he stood in front of the band looking a lot like his close friend Salvador Dalí, waving a wand with one hand and holding a chihuahua in the other. Charo writhed and carried on at a spot front and center. They were a Latin Ike and Tina.

That's where the resemblance ended. According to Charo, their partnership was all strictly business. Once she got away from Cugat and made some talk show appearances on her own, Spanish lightning struck. She became an in-demand guest on everything and would end up sailing on *The Love Boat* (1977–1987) eleven times, always as Charo, or something so close to Charo, you might as well call it Charo. But even before she set sail, her popularity inevitably led to someone coming up with a bold idea: Charo in a sitcom. Developed for ABC, it was called *Charo and the Marine*, later changed to *Charo and the Sergeant*. *Charo and the Marine* might have been a title for a sex tape; it has a certain ring. So the title change happened early.

The idea was Charo would be Charo. You can't fight that. In a classic comedy setup, this flamboyant, irrepressible personality marries a straitlaced, conservative, *ooo-rah* US Marine sergeant, lives on the base, and generally wreaks havoc with the plain, simple citizens around her. The husband loves her but objects to everything she does. But the fish out of water aspect of Charo's show wore thin before the half hour was over. So the pilot didn't go.

But Fred Silverman, who has visited these pages already, was running ABC at the time, and he believed in Charo. Instead of making her a fish out of water, he put her in the pond where she belonged and invited us to dive in with her. In the new show—cunningly titled *Charo*—Charo would play Charo, just like Jack Benny played Jack Benny. Like Jack, Charo would live in Beverly Hills—she actually did live around the corner from him—and like Jack, she would go into a studio every week to do a variety show: part sketches, part musical numbers. There would be a guest star playing themselves, and part of the show would take place at home and part onstage and backstage. It really *was* the Jack Benny show. Like Jack at home, Charo at home would still be Charo, who always related to the world as if she were onstage and on fire.

This kind of show required a team of writers to commit. This was where I met producers Bob Booker and George Foster, the two guys with whom I subsequently committed *The Paul Lynde Halloween Special*. True to form, they corralled a weird quartet of writers to come up with stuff. It was as diverse as most writers' rooms were in that day, three men and one woman, and we were all Jewish. The only person involved with the show who spoke Spanish was Charo, and at lunchtime, Irma, who pulled her taco truck up to the door of the studio. Irma and Charo didn't have much to say to each other in any language. Charo ate food she prepared herself in between practicing guitar.

Two of the writers were certifiably brilliant people. Sybil Adelman is a genuine wit, and she was part of a circle of spectacular women writers like Barbara Gallagher (original *SNL*), Iris Rainer (*Beaches*) and Lynn Roth (stay tuned, I've got a story right after this one). Rubin Carson was a genius and certifiably insane. He wasn't a comedy writer per se; I think he was a friend of Booker and Foster, but he was what used to be called a humorist, writing hilarious essays and satires and occasionally a script. He was also a foodie, writing reviews

If you don't
recognize her,
she's holding a
script that tells
all. I am wearing
a mildly obscene
T-shirt.

for various Los Angeles media, and into all of his stuff he managed to
insert updates on his tumultuous family life, which he called *Scenes
from a Valley Marriage.*

The joke machine known as Jeffrey Barron was a stogie-smoking
one-liner sharpshooter who wrote for Bob Hope and a lot of other
comics when he wasn't at the track losing the money they all paid him.

Jeffrey took all kinds of work, and if he didn't like the show, he would use his nom de plume in the credits. One day his accountant called to tell him his nom de plume was making more money than he was.

Jeffrey was friendly with the dean of the joke writers, Harry Crane, who dropped by one day to look at the four Jews writing for the Spanish lady. He asked Jeffrey if he was going to go the nom de plume route on this one and was surprised when Jeffrey said no. Harry said he never used a nom de plume. He said if he didn't like the show he was working on, he would take his paycheck and put it on the passenger seat of his Cadillac. He would then go for a ride, stop at a light, look at people waiting for the bus, look at the check, and start singing "Zip-a-dee-doo-dah!" at top volume. It worked even better if it was raining.

Jeffrey and I were both friendly with comedy legend Henny Youngman, who we'd met on one show or another. I once asked Henny if he ever did private shows and he said yes; for a thousand bucks he would show up and do ten minutes.

On Jeffrey's birthday, I threw a little dinner party in my apartment. Midway through the salad, the doorbell rang. I asked Jeffrey to get it. He opened the door and Henny was standing there, in a tuxedo with his fiddle. He said, "Happy birthday, Jeffrey. Guy walks into a psychiatrist's office, says nobody ever listens to me, psychiatrist says—'Next!'" (Quick fiddling of "Smoke Gets in Your Eyes.") "Marriage is complicated. Take my wife—please!" Ten minutes later he looked at his watch. "Well, that's my time. Happy birthday, Jeffrey." And off he went.

On the pilot episode, we were hoping for a guest star who could play comedy, maybe do something musical with Charo, and be a willing accomplice in whatever cock-a-bally (my mother's favorite term for horseshit) we cooked up. What we got was Mike Connors—Mannix, the stolid, stone-faced private eye, on another network, no less. He was a big TV name at the time, but I never understood why we couldn't find somebody more . . . I guess *show bizzy* would be the way to describe it.

That could be because, like certain kinds of cheese, Charo stood alone. You didn't need anybody else onstage with her. You needed an audience she could play with, but this wasn't that kind of show. I will say Mike Connors was game. He played the Big Star neighbor who was going to be on the show doing sketches, so we had him dropping in on her at home and then we got to do a sketch with the two of them as George and Martha Washington, for reasons I have blocked like an artery.

On the musical front, we had Frank De Vol, the celebrated arranger-conductor who had worked with everybody, as Charo's musical director and friend. Frank worked as just De Vol, which Charo immediately turned into De Ball. You could write a straight line and watch her turn it into a comic line with a simple mispronunciation. To this day, she says she doesn't understand American politics, with the Republicans and the Democraps.

Things were going swimmingly until one day we were told Charo wasn't coming in because she had to go to city hall. I thought maybe she was cutting a ribbon, or rebuilding Chavez Ravine, but it turns out that she said that there was a typo on her citizenship documents that she wished to have fixed. It said she was born in 1941. In fact, she said she was born in 1951. The problem was the hall of records in the town outside Madrid where she was born . . . burned down. And all the records were, well, need I finish that sentence? So she brought her entire family, now relocated from Spain, into the records office here to swear oaths that she was born in 1951. I believe several of them changed their own birth dates as well. It was a big fire.

It apparently also consumed all of Charo's childhood photos. Or maybe that was another fire. The whole thing started when we asked her to give us some photos of her as a kid for a joke we wanted to do where we would doctor all of them so that little Charo had huge hair, huge boobs, lots of sequins, and a face full of makeup, even if she was in gym class. That was when we found out about the crispy photos. However old she is, she's golden. And she was back after lunch to continue hazing Mike Connors, who was having a good time, or at least an unusual one.

We had all been told the show was a pilot for the series that would take the slot intended for *Charo and the Sergeant*, but when the show finally aired—some months after we shot it, not standard for variety—we were told it was a stand-alone special. The irony was we were a ratings hit. Our principal competition was *The John Davidson Show*, a variety hour on NBC that did well, but not well enough that you've heard of it. Charo's agents bought a full-page ad in the trade papers claiming CHARO IS MAGIC! But she's not the one who made the show disappear.

From what I heard, the marketing people came to the conclusion that we all had arrived at on *día numero uno*. Charo is a special. Whether people would tune in every week to see her antics was another matter. Often in these cases, the network sniffs around the advertising community to see what their hunch is, and often it doesn't go the way you would like it to go. Did I mention—it seemed like a bad idea at the time?

I did mention Lynn Roth before, and some years later, she was a part of another bad idea that, truthfully, was a good idea when we started, and got shot down for the most amazing reason. First, a little background. *The Golden Girls* (1985–1992) is one of the biggest comedy hits of all time, still in reruns on numerous platforms. I was not surprised, as everyone I know who had a mother in Florida, including me, had pitched the idea of a bunch of widows sharing a condo. Only Susan Harris, the brilliant creator of *Soap* (1977–1981), had managed to snare two and a half huge TV names—Bea Arthur, Betty White, and Rue McClanahan—to be in her show. She almost had Elaine Stritch, but Elaine told that story better than anyone else could, and it's on tape.

Susan's script was terrific. The show took off like a rocket not financed by Elon Musk. Suddenly, every older actress who felt her career had been reduced to being slaughtered by a serial killer in the first reel of a slasher picture was in demand—if she was funny. One of those, and one who really wanted it bad, was Carol Channing.

Some might say she was too big for the small screen, perhaps even too big for the seventy-two-inchers everyone now has on their living room wall, but no matter. America loved her—she was the star of the first Super Bowl halftime show! Carol's good friend was Barbara Walters, and Barbara's husband at the time was Merv Adelson, who was running Lorimar, then a major supplier of television programming. So Merv sent forth the word that he was looking for a vehicle for Carol.

I had written for Carol's act and a lot of special material for the many benefits for AIDS charities and others that she was doing. Her husband-manager, Charles Lowe, thought I should write the show. People in the sitcom business suggested I partner with someone who knew the sitcom form, as I had never concentrated on that area. When they suggested Lynn Roth, I jumped at it. Smart, witty, accomplished, and a woman, which I thought would be very helpful for Carol. Many times in the dark, departed days of television comedy, a female star was surrounded by men and often felt ganged up on. Having a force like Lynn in the room would be invaluable. Plus, Lynn is a funny writer, and she gets comic actors and their needs.

We had dinner with Carol and Charles. Dinner with those two was almost always a carbon copy of the scene in the second act of *Hello, Dolly!* when Dolly sits down with her mark, Horace, at the Harmonia Gardens and eats a pheasant. Charles and Carol had been together for at least thirty years at this point. I got a big kick out of Charles. He would call people up and start the conversation with "This is Charles Lowe, Carol Channing's husband." I was amazed he had the self-worth to do that. "Saves time" was his explanation.

Sometime after they were married, Carol developed some food allergies and she had to be very careful with her diet. Charles bought farms where her food was grown, and anytime you went to dinner with them, Carol had a designer bag full of Tiffany sterling thermoses with her. We had dinner once at Chasen's, where jackets and ties were required of the gentlemen, and Carol called to tell me to wear a jacket over my usual T-shirt—she had it all covered. I arrived as she did and we walked in together. She was wearing a suit and tie. "Pretend he's the woman," she said to the maître d', and before I could work up a joke, we were seated.

The dinner to discuss the show was at the Lowe home in Birdland, that part of Hollywood Hills where all the streets are named after our feathered friends who survived the Hitchcock picture. Warbler Way was the address. Just west of Oriole and near Mockingbird. I always wanted a house on Swallow Drive, but some other bird beat me to it.

It wasn't really their house—they didn't have a house, they lived in hotels (in New York, the Waldorf Towers). In L.A., they crashed at the home of Wallace Seawell, an MGM portrait photographer who became Carol's road manager for her concert act. He trekked around the world with a box of fake diamond rings she would throw into the crowd while singing "Diamonds Are a Girl's Best Friend," the song she'd introduced on Broadway in the original 1949 production of *Gentlemen Prefer Blondes*. When they were in town, they took over Wally's house, but he didn't mind a bit. They were family. More than that, I was afraid to contemplate. The garage was permanently occupied by Carol's Rolls-Royce, which was dutifully trucked out for all appearances in town.

Wally made dinner for and Lynn and me, who were accompanied by Barnet Kellman, a director who was having a big hit with *Murphy Brown* and had been tipped to Carol and Charles as the man for this job. It was the Harmonia Gardens again. Wally and Charles kept jumping up and serving things, phones were ringing, Carol did a nonstop monologue while spooning things out of her thermos. I wondered if we could get all this energy into our show, but it would be exhausting every episode.

Barnet went back to *Murphy*, and Lynn and I spent some time figuring out exactly what sort of human being Carol could play. She was a legendary performer and a smart, strong actress, believe it or not, but the two roles with which she was identified in the public's mind were Lorelei Lee in *Gentlemen Prefer Blondes* and Dolly Levi in *Hello, Dolly!* It was to Carol's great chagrin that those parts were swiped from her for the movies by Marilyn Monroe and Barbra Streisand. Undaunted, she continued to play them onstage until the very end. She did two different versions of Lorelei on Broadway and endless tours of Dolly everywhere. A brief detour into *Thoroughly Modern Millie* (1967) got her an Oscar nomination, but it was essentially Lorelei after she'd finally gotten some money.

Both Lorelei and Dolly were stories of gold diggers, one a traditional young one and the other a middle-aged one who wanted to live well for a change before the parade passed her by. We didn't think the story of a gold digger would have a lot of appeal on a weekly basis. So we landed on another trope: a rich woman whose husband dies and she discovers there's no money. Eerily, this presaged what happened to Carol when Charles got sick and eventually died, but at the moment, it seemed like a good way to give a character a motivation for getting out of bed every morning and creating a life for herself.

We made her a hostess in Washington, DC, taking the same cue from socialite Perle Mesta that Irving Berlin took for *Call Me Madam*. Her husband had been a prominent lobbyist and she entertained lavishly. In our pilot, she's come home from the funeral to discover things being repossessed. Comic license! After going through a memorial service where she has to keep up appearances, she realizes her only way out is to do what she knows she can do best: throw parties. So she becomes a party coordinator, event planner, caterer. The supporting cast are all the people she works with, as her disapproving children only show up to tell her they want no part of it. Conflict!

My mother had been a party coordinator as a side hustle. A doctor's wife, she wanted her own thing besides his. We named the show after her. *Henne*. Carol loved that and she thought it was a good omen. I shoulda known then.

Off we went to write the script, and off she went to dental surgery. A few weeks later, we delivered. Lorimar loved it. CBS, which had bought the idea from Lorimar, loved it. Barnet loved it. Charles loved it. Everybody was so pleased that this could be a new direction for Carol.

She hated it.

We never knew why. She didn't like this woman, was all she said to me, and she never said why. We had crafted it for her, playing to all her strengths, but she didn't see it that way.

And then it occurred to me that her two signature roles were not written for her; she got to make them her own. This was written for her based on things we knew she could play, and she didn't like what she saw. Maybe we put in all the tricks she was supposed to discover for herself. We never got a rational explanation. And maybe there wasn't one. Maybe she was just terrified to do something new. What if it failed? That had happened to her more than once, but not in this arena. I asked Charles and he shrugged and said, "Sometimes she's crazy."

Oddly enough, I wound up writing a few little benefit pieces for her later, and we remained friends until her death in 2019. Not so Charles. He had a stroke, and that began a protracted battle over money and control and a long, sad story, the only bright part being when Carol sued for divorce in 1998 and claimed they had only had sex two times in forty years.

I said she should write a book and call it *Twice Upon a Mattress*.

She laughed louder than she did at anything in the script.

10

Oscar! Oscar! (1989)

Or, at Least Nobody Sued...
Oh, Wait a Minute, Somebody Did

During the last writers' strike, a friend of mine posted a message on social media, or as it is known at my man cave, keyboard warfare, saying how it would be fine with him if all awards shows were done without writers, thus sparing us all the "witless banter and egregious propagandizing" that is "inevitably" a part of such proceedings. I immediately blocked him and his agent, who had undoubtedly pitched him to write on one of my awards shows.

I then realized that in some quarters, awards shows are considered the bad ideas of all time. It follows that the Academy Awards, the biggest of them, would therefore be the worst. It doesn't really follow, but please play along.

The Oscars are the awards show that started it all. They're creeping up on one hundred years of thanking the little people, and even in a world of diminished ratings, they still pull in more eyeballs than any of the others.

I have been officially credited on twenty-five of them, and unofficially involved with a dozen more. Sometimes I was the head writer, sometimes I was on the team that wrote for the host, sometimes the team that wrote for everyone *but* the host, sometimes straddling the two teams like Yakima Canutt driving a runaway stagecoach. Also sometimes phoning it in as a favor to a friend who needed a rewrite. Translation: uncredited.

I've won two Emmys for cowriting two of the Oscar shows hosted by Billy Crystal, and was nominated for the Steve Martin–Alec Baldwin show, and probably should have been nominated for a few others, but the writers who nominate suffer from Oscar fatigue just like everybody else, and it's difficult to compete with a popular comedian who's written a terrific stand-up special. My mother got confused now and again on whether I won an Oscar for writing the Emmys or was it the other way round. You can't win an Oscar for writing the Emmys, and you can't win an Emmy for writing the Emmys, either, because even the Television Academy recognizes how infra dig and crazy meta that would be.

Onstage rehearsing at an awards show whose set I don't recognize. Proof that they are all a little bit alike.

I'm back. Had to lie down after that paragraph.

The first Oscar show I got to have my name on is the most infamous: the Snow White show, 1989. The same Allan Carr who fired me off the Village People picture came to me ten years later and asked me to write the Academy Awards, which he was entrusted to overhaul with his big-time showman ways. Allan could sell something like nobody else. He sold *me* on writing the show, previously written by several teams of writers, by myself. Never having done an awards show before, I had no idea what a foolhardy proposition that was. And I didn't remain alone for long. We roped Hildy Parks, writer of many great Tony Awards shows, to partner with me.

Allan also sold the Academy on a few other things. He had them sit down with the L.A. municipal government and formulate a strategic traffic plan so that the parade of limos heading for the Shrine Auditorium could coexist with Los Angeles rush hour traffic. Allan loathed seeing a star in traffic-produced distress.

He engaged Fred Hayman, grand pooh-bah of Giorgio, the toniest dress shop in Beverly Hills, as "fashion consultant," and organized a preshow fashion event to whet everyone's appetite. The Oscars are as much about dresses as movies, why not admit that? He got some corporations to design and cater the greenroom backstage so overdressed divas could canoodle in comfort before their appearances onstage.

Instead of a host, he came up with the creative theme of presenters who had a reason to be onstage together, either as real-life couples (Jeff Goldblum and Geena Davis, Melanie Griffith and Don Johnson), movie pairs (Kim Novak and James Stewart, Sammy Davis Jr. and Gregory Hines), or colleagues (two James Bonds, Sean Connery and Roger Moore, with Michael Caine, all three of whom would later be knighted, but not for this).

To beef up the marquee, he added clips of the five nominated best pictures, each introduced by a movie star. At the suggestion of the new director, Jeff Margolis, he changed "The winner is . . ." is to

"And the Oscar goes to . . ."—a kinder, gentler way of covering the strained expressions of goodwill that form on the faces of the people who don't win.

Allan knew he could sell better than anyone. Unfortunately, he also thought he could write better than anyone, direct better than anyone, edit better than anyone, design better than anyone. He believed that passing judgment on other people's work was the same as creating that work. This was unfortunate, as it alienated other people, even his own management client, Marvin Hamlisch, who was the music director for the show and finally had to say to him, "Allan, I know what I'm doing."

I had not reached that august level with him, but he didn't give me too much of a hard time, because he was so busy marketing the event. And that was something he could do better than anybody else. In his non-Oscar life, he drove around in a yellow Mercedes convertible that was a gift from Universal for showing them how to sell *The Deer Hunter* (1978), which they had more or less given up on as a lost downer. Allan saw a screening of it and was profoundly moved and laid out a marketing plan that worked beyond all of their dreams. In the smoke of what has been written about Allan, his real talents have become invisible.

Meanwhile, I was getting to write for giants I had worshipped: Jack Lemmon and Walter Matthau, Lucille Ball and Bob Hope. It was the last appearance Lucille made before her startling death a month later. She and Hope introduced a number that was so strange it made people almost forget their appearance a minute before.

It happened because, in Allan's view, the entries that were eligible for the Best Original Song award were so uninteresting to him, and so unheard (not a good thing for a song), that he got the music branch to institute a minimum number of votes a song had to get in order to make the top five. Only three songs reached it, so only three were nominated. One by Phil Collins, one by Carly Simon, and one by Bob Telson. I know, I haven't come across that last name lately, either, but it was the song from the West German dramedy *Bagdad Cafe*, sung by Oleta Adams.

Phil Collins was, we heard, pissed at the Academy for not asking him to perform his nominated song in a previous year, turning it instead into an interpretive ballet for Ann Reinking. So Phil was out. Carly Simon was in a period of not performing live, so that was two strikes. Oleta Adams, who is a gorgeous vocalist, was not the draw Allan was looking for, and no one else was interested in performing either of the other songs, so the music branch allowed Allan to, for the one and only time, cut the original song performances altogether.

Instead, Allan had two unrelated musical numbers up his sleeve, one of which became the modern definition of infamy. It was the other one that Hope and Lucille introduced. These two famous movie partners and stratospheric television stars liked what I wrote for them, and I remember after they rehearsed it, Lucille said to me, "I like it and I'll do it just like that, but he'll do whatever he wants to do, you know that, don't you?" Ultimately, it didn't matter—the crowd ate them up. They feasted on the number that followed, but for all the wrong reasons.

Allan, starstruck to a fault, decided it would be great fun to do the ultimate nepo-baby production, and that term would not be invented for thirty more years. He made a list of all of the kids of all the famous Hollywood people he could think of and canvassed the bunch to see who could sing, who could dance, who could do neither but looked pretty. It was an eclectic group. Connie Stevens's two daughters by Eddie Fisher, Joely Fisher and Tricia Leigh Fisher, came along, as did Tyrone Power Jr., Keith Coogan (grandson of Jackie), Carrie Hamilton (daughter of Carol Burnett), Tracy Nelson (daughter of Ricky and granddaughter of Ozzie and Harriet!), and Patrick O'Neal, son of Ryan but not an Oscar winner like his half sister Tatum, who wisely passed. Less intuitively, participants also included Chad Lowe (brother of Rob;

more to come on him), Patrick Dempsey and Corey Parker (Patrick was married to Corey's mother Rocky, his much older manager), Corey Feldman (an unrelated Corey), Ricki Lake and Savion Glover (I was never sure of their status in the theme of things), Christian Slater (mother was in casting), Holly Robinson (mother was a manager), and Matt Lattanzi (wife was Olivia Newton-John). Forgive me if I've left out any member of Young Hollywood. The number, written by John Kander and Fred Ebb (also not in the Broadway production of their *New York, New York*) and arranged and conducted by Marvin Hamlisch, was called "I Wanna Be an Oscar Winner," and, to date, none of them has become one.

It was a very elaborate production on one of those enormous staircases you've seen in every old Hollywood musical ever, and solos flew by as you tried to identify who everybody was. The only spot I remember was Patrick Dempsey's; he proved to be an adept Gene Kelly dancer, lithe and graceful and totally in control of his hat.

The other number that Allan came up with was the one that has the distinction of being the *Titanic* of TV production numbers, the one that sank on its maiden voyage and remains a subject of passionate interest thirty-five years later. To date, nobody has made a movie about it, but streaming has a hearty appetite that must be appeased, and I wouldn't rule it out.

It started, as the Village People movie started ten years earlier, with Allan seeing a performance. I wasn't there for this one, but he called, abrim with enthusiasm, to tell me about it. It was in San Francisco, and it was called *Beach Blanket Babylon*.

The *Beach Blanket* shows started in 1974, created by a dynamo named Steve Silver and maintained by his wife, later widow, Jo. Many times, San Francisco show biz types have said to me, "In this town, if it ain't flashin', they don't see it." The *Beach Blanket* shows flashed like the beacon on Telegraph Hill, beckoning all the ships at sea. Stuffed into the top floor of a union hall, or something like it, in

North Beach, the haunt of beatnik poets and filmmakers, it told the story of Snow White's trip around the world in eighty ways.

This mock Disney Candide-ette met every bizarre experience, including impersonations of famous people dead and alive, with wide-eyed innocence and lunatic happiness. Many of them featured mammoth headdresses they could *just* keep from plummeting into the ringside patrons. Snow wound up in San Francisco, of course, with a massive gondola on her head containing the entire city skyline, the Golden Gate Bridge, that beacon, everything but Kim Novak, Jeanette MacDonald, and Carol Doda.* It was quintessentially San Francisco, risqué but innocent, satirical but fun loving, the message being *Come here and be yourself, whatever you are.* It was the kind of thing that local audiences embraced and tourists enjoyed for its uniqueness. It never really worked anywhere else. They tried it in London and Vegas. But it was a fish out of water wherever it went . . . as Allan Carr was about to demonstrate on global television.

Allan's bad idea was to take Snow White to Hollywood and the Oscars. This, of course, took her out of her context. What reason did Snow White have to return to Hollywood? Steve Silver had never considered featuring it in her world tour, maybe because he planted Hollywood characters in all the places she visited. Also the show was San Francisco–centric. So to have Snow White come back to Hollywood would beg the question: Why? Having her dance down the aisle at the Shrine would be a real disruptor. Iceberg, dead ahead.

To add to the confusion, Snow would wind up at a reincarnation of L.A.'s Cocoanut Grove nightclub, and to further add to the incongruity, the room would be stacked with stars from Snow White's own golden age. Allan made up a list of stars who would be seated there.

---

* Three San Francisco monuments: Kim starring in Hitchcock's SF-set *Vertigo*, Jeanette singing "San Francisco" as the town crumbled around her in the film of the same name, and Carol the topless North Beach tassel-twirler who took stripping to the next level.

What he failed or willfully refused to take into account was that his memory of the stars he loved as a teenager did not stack up with the condition they were in today, 1989. Lower all boats.

He plunged ahead with the number. As it was set at the Cocoanut Grove, Merv Griffin was enlisted to pretend he was the boy singer on the bandstand, as he once had been, singing "I've Got a Lovely Bunch of Coconuts," which may have been the moment that caused one homophobic critic to write that the number simulated a gay nightclub. Maybe it was the other bits from *Babylon* that were peppered throughout the thing.

One wholly original piece never made it past dress rehearsal: an unlikely trio made up of Mayim Bialik and the Nicholas Brothers. Mayim at the time was a child actress with her *Big Bang Theory* and *Jeopardy!* days far ahead of her. At the moment, she was noted for playing Bette Midler as a little girl in *Beaches*. Harold and Fayard Nicholas were a dance team noted for coming down a staircase by doing a split on each step and for flying across the stage in superhuman style. As old as they were—sixty-eight and seventy-four—they could still do it, and with relative ease. The routine that had been cooked up for them and young Mayim was a knockoff of the things little Shirley Temple did with Bill "Bojangles" Robinson in musicals of the '30s, things that younger viewers only knew from Carol Burnett sketches. It was fun to watch these three carry on, but as the whole opening shebang was heading toward thirty minutes of airtime, something had to go, and the axe wound up falling on them. They got off the boat just in time.

The thing that stayed, and stayed, and stayed was not that trio but another trio, the trio that would not die . . . Snow White and Rob Lowe and "Proud Mary." Rob has written and spoken and podcasted about this calamity, and Michael Schulman, in his excellent book *Oscar Wars*, unearthed Eileen Bowman, the young performer who played Snow White and had quite a story to tell, but here's what I know.

First off, Hildy Parks and I had nothing to do with the number.

It was crafted by Steve Silver and Allan Carr and all we could do was offer opinions that, if they didn't concur with Allan's, were dismissed after ten seconds like the pasties on Carol Doda.

As it finally turned out, the number began at the end of the red carpet arrivals, which had yet to blossom into the full-scale "What are you wearing?" fashion parade that now upstages the movies. As tradition dictated, *Variety* columnist Army Archerd conducted a series of mini interviews with legends and newcomers, the last one being something of both: Snow White, in the person of Miss Bowman, playing her as directed, just like she would be played in the *Beach Blanket* show. But she wasn't there. She was at the Academy Awards and coming down the aisle seeing and talking to famous people who were not exactly ready to see and talk to her. Some were pros and played along, some were too nervous, some couldn't quite put together what was happening. None had been warned. Some faces reflected a common feeling: *I am nominated for an Academy Award and I'm suddenly a day player in somebody else's movie?* The terror was only beginning.

She mounted the stage and the curtain rose to reveal the Cocoanut Grove and Merv, and several tables of . . . who are they, exactly, I'm not sure I recognize them? There was Cyd Charisse, looking great, and Alice Faye, looking well, and Roy Rogers and Dale Evans, in full cowboy drag, smiling up a storm. But when Dorothy Lamour was gingerly moved downstage by two chorus boys manfully holding each arm, it was not a good look. These were not the golden stars we remembered, and this was not the glamorous Hollywood look Allan had been going for.

He watched it in his office, in tears. He idolized these people so. And he had gotten his wish, but he had deluded himself into thinking he had pulled it off. Then along came Mary.

As an antidote to the admitted antiquarian head count onstage, a young, hot presence was needed to perform with Snow White, and after a number of people politely declined, the good-natured,

I'll-try-anything Rob Lowe stepped in. Not famous for singing or danc-ing but for being pretty, which was an overriding qualification here, Rob grabbed a microphone and launched into "Proud Mary." The song had nothing to do with Hollywood, nothing to do with anything nominated that year, nothing to do with Rob Lowe or Snow White, but there it was, opening the greatest show on earth and your TV.

People had very strong reactions, one of which we will get to in a moment, but while they were forming them, it was left to my friend and colleague Lily Tomlin to welcome everyone, in the absence of a host.

Lily and I had sat watching the dress rehearsal with a small bunch of people who, when the song finished, all looked at each other like the stagehands high above Citizen Kane's mistress when she sang grand opera. We knew the ship of show was very much down at the head and taking water.

Lily asked, "How do I follow that?" I told her it would be funny if, coming down the giant staircase, one of her shoes came off and she had to limp downstage. There was no time for her to rehearse that safely, so instead we got a stagehand to place a stray shoe on the stairs as if it had come off someone's foot during the number, and then had another stagehand crawl down from the top of the staircase to get it as if hoping nobody would notice, while Lily made her wel-coming remarks. We thought it would take the audience's mind off what they had just seen and give her something to play with. All the lines we wrote about what a spectacle we had all just witnessed were as double-edged as a Delphic sword. I think Lily emerged unscathed, and we were into a commercial, about which more in a minute.

The show resumed with the president of the Academy making the speech that you can't seem to talk presidents of the Academy out of making. You know, film is the universal language, those beautiful people out there in the dark, more people are watching this show than there are on this or any neighboring planet, and so on.

And then the first presenters came out, Melanie Griffith and Don

Johnson, and did a very funny bit giving the Supporting Actress award to Geena Davis for *The Accidental Tourist*. The show ran pretty well after that.

There were a couple of bits that I liked that other people pointedly didn't. Bruce Willis and Demi Moore, presenting Cinematography, showed home movies of their new baby as an example of *bad* cinematography. Martin Short and Carrie Fisher showed up each wearing the same dress ("Carrie, you have hundreds of dresses. I have four"), and Kurt Russell went off the *printed* script to do a bit where he sort of proposed to an allegedly unprepared Goldie Hawn. This last became a tabloid favorite in the pre-internet universe; it made covers all over the world.

The James Bonds were charming, and Jimmy Stewart and Kim Novak had fun giving the Sound award, with Jimmy exaggerating his drawling speech, which he said drove the sound people crazy. Candice Bergen and Jackie Bisset introduced the Foreign Film award partly in French, then were joined by Jack Valenti, Hollywood's ambassador in Washington, who admitted he didn't speak it. Billy Crystal did a hilarious piece, and Patrick Swayze did a tender tribute to his inspiration as a kid, the big Hollywood musicals.

Watching all this from home was the titular head of the Walt Disney Company, one Frank Wells, an old Hollywood corporate hand, and Frank was not amused. The outcome of his non-amusement has echoed through the corridors of gossip. Here is what I know, or was told, by several sources at the time.

At the time, the Academy had a policy of not allowing commercial spots for movies to be a part of the broadcast, thinking that it would imply endorsement by the Academy, especially since so many commercials used phrases like "Oscar winner," "Oscar nominee," etc. For reasons no one has explained to me, this fiat had been expanded to include such things as theme parks run by members of the Academy. Disney was about to open what was then called the Disney-MGM

Studios at Walt Disney World, now known as Disney's Hollywood Studios. They wanted to advertise it on the Oscars, but they apparently got a *no*. So they made a deal with Chevrolet to film their introduction of a new-model Chevy at the new park, in the forecourt of its imitation Grauman's Chinese Theatre. They wanted to show us how big the car was, so guess who popped out of it . . . Snow White and the Seven Dwarfs. Frank Wells went ballistic. He started calling people during the show to complain.

I'm guessing he was mad because our Snow White made his commercial's Snow White look like sloppy seconds . . . who may have been the eighth dwarf, by the way. The wheels went into motion. I don't think he knew beforehand about our opening number, but here's who did: the lawyers at Disney, who, even though Snow White is in the public domain and they have no rights in the matter, signed off on the look of our Snow. Also the lawyers at the Academy and at the network that aired the show, ABC, both of whom were consulted. There was a Snow White Cafe on Hollywood Boulevard that everyone in Hollywood had been to or at least knew about, and it remained in operation until 2024, and nobody ever blasted them publicly for copyright infringement.

The Academy was, of course, loath to get into a copyright or trademark dispute with one of its own members, especially as the Oscar trademark is its prime, heavily defended asset. So the next day they issued an apology, cut the number from the archival tape, and thought it was settled. For the moment, peace was on the land.

While all this was hatching, I accompanied Allan in his limo to the shindig being thrown by Irving Lazar, known as Swifty to the world, the legendary power agent whose Oscar-night viewing party at the old Spago restaurant was the annual hot ticket (it has been replaced by the *Vanity Fair* party and an explosion of other parties around town). Allan thought the show had gone well, and after the opening number, it had, in the theater. The nation had not yet checked in.

But he was a little despondent and at a disturbingly low energy level, for him. He looked out the window at the freeway and quietly said, "I burned a lot of bridges on this one."

He was right, starting with the people who had produced previous shows, whom he'd dumped all over in the press and trash-talked around town in the run-up to the show. Then there were the people who assumed they would be on the show but were not asked—or, even worse, were asked and then unasked because the network had told him he had to "young up" the proceedings. The day after the show, a couple of those people wrote a letter to the Academy about the show they were not asked to be on. They got many famous people to sign the letter, which a lot of them turned out to have never read. These were all friends of Allan's, at least in his mind.

The press, who had not been in the room where it happened, did not care for the show either, and gave Allan a major shellacking. This was the same press he had spent his entire career lavishly courting, the press who he also thought were his friends. Allan never recovered. As producer Gil Cates, with whom I did a lot of subsequent Oscar shows, put it, "All a producer really has is his taste. When that's invalidated, the game is over."

And then, only two months later, just when we were all beginning to put the show behind us, came the Rob Lowe Sex Tape.

Rob, who has long owned his mistake and has publicly called himself the poster child for bad choices, had taped himself having sex with a sixteen-year-old girl in a hotel room in Atlanta, where he was in town for the Democratic National Convention that nominated Michael Dukakis in 1988. Before viral was invented, this went viral. And every time it was mentioned, it was this: "Rob Lowe, most recently seen dancing with Snow White in a number on the Oscars that drew a lawsuit from the Walt Disney Company . . ."

The combination of the lawsuit and the letter and the sex tape sealed the show's fate in the Ninth Circle of Show Business Hell.

For all this, the show did exceptionally well in the Nielsen ratings, and people continue to tell me how, opening number aside, they enjoy watching it on You Tube—where the opening number exists, by the way.

The following year, the Oscars did a housecleaning, bringing in Gil Cates to replace Allan. I was persona non grata as well, but after a year of penance, Gil and host Billy Crystal brought me back into the fold, where I remained for . . . another book . . . this one about the shows that worked!

Coda

Or, at Least They Were the Worst

You might have noticed that all of the bad ideas mentioned so far have one thing in common. They were somebody else's. But I couldn't let you get away without telling you about one, just one, bad idea that was mine.

Actually, it may not have been mine, but I'd been thinking about it for years, and when the opportunity came up, I acted on it. Which was a bad idea. Maybe.

People had been telling me for years that I would be the perfect host for a late-night talk show. I never took them seriously; I thought it was . . . a bad idea. Until somebody offered me one. Now, I'm fun at a dinner party and I have hosted many benefits, but having a nightly monologue and doing comedic bits and interviewing guests who may or may not be of any real interest to me did not strike me as something I could pull off with a national audience five nights a week. Again, until somebody offered me the chance. Suddenly, I was thinking, *Why not?* Somebody else's interest awakened a desire in me I never realized I had. I think this is what leads a lot of creative people into the Valley of Bad Decisions. Somebody will pay me to do this? Well . . . why not?

It was around the end of the last century and I was being seen nightly on *Hollywood Squares*—where if you're lucky, you get to do two or three jokes a show—so I was a bona fide TV personality. The offer came from the cable channel Bravo, which had originally been positioned as a showcase for the performing arts—hence the name. The channel-runners were just starting to put their big toe into more commercial waters, and one of the things that appealed to them was the idea of a late-night talk show that they could marry to their brand. So they commissioned three different hosts to shoot three different pilots. I was one of them.

The show was to be produced by World of Wonder, the company that was making its bones (and a helluva lotta cash) on RuPaul and documentaries about Tammy Faye Bakker. Fortunately, the RuPaul spirit prevailed here. Bravo was looking for a semi-conventional but wacky take on the talk show format. If you've ever seen Eric André's show on Adult Swim, you get the idea. There's a desk and a couch and strange things happen. We couldn't stray as far as Eric, as that might scare the audience, and nobody in mainstream television wants to do that, unless they call it *American Horror Story*.

So our set for the pilot had a desk and a couch. And the desk was in the shape of a huge cheesecake, in honor of one of my favorite things that's no good for me. Actually, the entire set looked like a Candy Land smack dream. I came out and did something I never really had done before, although I'd worked on hundreds of them for others—a monologue.

This was all-new turf for me. As I used to say at the top of my cabaret act, "I have no act." In my cabaret appearances, I told stories about my life in show business and newspapers. It was topical to a degree, but to come out and do a sample monologue about the news of a sample day was daunting. People who host late-night talk shows have comic personae they have honed over years of work, either as performers or writers. Many years later, I marveled at how a gifted actor turned talk show host like James Corden could come out and do political jokes like he'd been doing them all his life. Was he acting? Notice that in spite of his success, he's not hosting anymore. He probably got tired of playing the role. Maybe that's what I was setting myself up for, and I couldn't figure out what role to play.

The audience laughed anyway, maybe because I was in a jewel-encrusted T-shirt that the great Bob Mackie had run up for me, and because they *did* know me from *Squares*. And because I was driven onto the set with much fanfare in a gold golf cart piloted by Kato Kaelin from the O. J. Simpson trial, with whom I flirted, and which put the seal of ridiculousness on the whole thing right from the start.

One of the things every talk show host needs is a sidekick, someone to play off of when things go well—or, even more crucially, when they don't. Usually they are the time-honored guys who announce the show. I don't think I've ever seen a female one. Fallon and Conan have straight men they kibbitz with. Corden and Colbert have musicians. Kimmel has his Latin page Guillermo, which verges on the ridiculous almost immediately. Seth Meyers generally goes it alone, except for the nights when he used to job in deadpan Fred Armisen to play in the band, who were later cut for costs. We decided to go a different route. We hired my mother.

My mother, Henne Vilanch, had made something of a splash in the documentary made about me in 1999, *Get Bruce*.* She and Robin Williams were the de facto stars of that picture, each getting laugh after laugh. My mother always wanted a career in show business, but she married a doctor and had a kid and settled into that life, exorcising her demons by performing at benefits and encouraging me to do the same. But she yearned for the spotlight. She was not an actress, but

---

* The documentary, made by the late Andrew Kuehn, was all about me but more interestingly a deconstruction of how comedy gets written. Robin Williams and my mother are the real stars, seriously. Produced by Harvey Weinstein, who never laid a hand on me. #WhyNotMe?

I'd once leaned on a friend who was a producer on *Law & Order* to get her a part. She would be the person who discovers the body in the first two minutes of the show. She had two lines, one of them a full-throated scream. When she found out how much it would cost to join the Screen Actors Guild, she politely declined the role. "Are you joking? I'm off the screen by 10:03!" Later, we got her on several years' worth of Mother's Day shows on *Hollywood Squares*, where she got to meet other celebrity mothers—which also got her a heavy discount at Joan Rivers's jewelry site. She would proudly frame her $1.86 residual checks and hang them where all the girls in the canasta game could ogle them. Being my sidekick would kick her career to another level.

While it wasn't a bad idea on the face of it, when we flew her out to California and did all those things to her that they did to Judy Garland in *A Star Is Born*—makeup, hair, wardrobe—she was another

Getting expert advice on playing Edna Turnblad in *Hairspray* from my mother, who was expert in everything.

person. So we got rid of all that and told her to just be herself. She was a delightful, entertaining individual, full of personality. But when she had to do it on cue, with lights and cameras and the knowledge that Everybody Would Be Watching . . . she froze. This made me overdo whatever I was doing in an effort to bring her out of her shell, something I had never, ever had to do in decades of being her son. The cheesecake began dripping flop sweat.

Luckily, we were taping the show and we had a lot of time. Nobody was expecting the thing to be ready by 11:30 that night. So we could do things over. But they didn't get any better. We had to move on. Once there were other people on the couch with her, she defrosted a bit, and by the end she was pretty much in the swing of it. I, of course, felt like I was the Norman Bates of talk show hosts, throwing my mother under the show biz bus and never looking back. But my guests snapped me back into why we were here.

I have to confess, it was a stellar group who answered the call: Debbie Reynolds, Tim Curry, and David Hyde Pierce. All old friends and colleagues, and they all came out and had a great time with each other on the couch, which was done up as some other kind of dessert. David and Tim were professional WASPs and classically trained, while Debbie's training was all at the MGM School of Hard Knocks, and it was wonderful to watch her break them up and them follow suit with her. I alternately thought, well, who wouldn't wanna watch *this* and . . . how do we do this every night? I guess that's how every talk show host starts their day, and it's a wonder they even bother to show up, knowing that it's like inventing the wheel every time.

I didn't have to worry about any of that. A few days after we delivered the pilot and broke up the cheesecake to live in various garages and spare rooms around town, somebody at Bravo reminded somebody else at Bravo that Bravo only had one feed, meaning that a show airing at 11:00 PM in New York was simultaneously airing at 8:00 PM in L.A. It would only be a late-night show on the East Coast.

Out here, it would be prime time. So all the crazy things they were imagining we could do would, they believed, not play well earlier in the evening. We never got the chance to prove them wrong, nor did the hosts of the other two pilots they simultaneously produced to throw against the wall to see which one stuck. Instead, they got reruns of *The West Wing*, very hot around the turn of the millennium. It helped that NBC bought Bravo in 2002 and could begin the repurposing of their old product, something that they have since honed to a high art with their streaming service Peacock. In 2004, Andy Cohen came in as Bravo's vice president of original programming and turned the channel into a Macy's parade of real housewives and residents of Kardashistan and Andy Cohen, culminating in 2019 with the first BravoCon, an event where everybody gets to touch a real housewife.

My mother was too real a housewife to ever be on any of those shows, but it didn't matter at that point. She put on a brave face, but I could tell it had been something of an ordeal for her, and with nothing to show the canasta game for all her trials. She soldiered on, but she didn't take it too seriously and she stopped asking me to get her parts on things. Like kung pao pork, it wasn't for her.

It clearly wasn't for me either. But for a minute, it had been a possibility . . . because I said yes. Nothing ever happens if you don't say yes, even if . . . it seems like a bad idea at the time.

Acknowledgments

I don't know exactly how you assemble a list of people to thank for helping you write some of the more legendary disasters in the history of show business. It's like giving each of them their own poster on Joe Allen's wall—a thank-you note they would have just as well not have received.

So look at it this way: Everybody who was involved in the catastrophes has been mentioned already, fair and foul. The following are the people who got me through them and helped me live to tell the story—and please, sing that last line as if Lin-Manuel Miranda wrote it.

The folks at Chicago Review Press who, to a Them, got Me: Jerome Pohlen, Connor Deeds, Melanie Roth, Cynthia Sherry, Cammie Fein, Candysse Miller, and especially my gracious and patient editor, Devon Freeny.

The stalwart individuals who handle my life: Jeremy Katz, Clay Mills, Jack Tantleff, Katelyn Dougherty, Anil Mohin, Tim and Roni Liddy, Robert Fromson, Carolyn Caroza, Jeanette Saylor, Dr. Barry Kohn, and Brina Kohn, a.k.a. the Queen of Portugal.

My support troops of long standing: Craig Austin, Matt Weiss, Matt Byars, Mark Cirillo, and the late Michael Wolf, fondly known to all as the Bitter Assistant.

Three guys who kept me working from the beginning: Adam Sher, the late Dan Stevens (not the actor, the agent masquerading as a Malibu beach bum), and George Lane, with whom I still share a birthday. And later, a few who gave me a performing career: John Moffitt and Pat Lee on TV and Jack O'Brien on Broadway.

My writing collaborators over the years, notably Jon Macks, Dave Boone, Patricia Resnick, Jerry Blatt, Bill Hennessy, Eric Kornfeld, Stephen Pouliot, Marilynn Preston, Beth Armogida, and the OGs Marc Shaiman and Scott Wittman . . . and the OOG, George Schlatter.

My family, who are all gone, and my newfound birth family, who have given me so much love and acceptance—and a medical history, goddammit.

The extraordinary talents whose genuine brilliance and depth of friendship have made my career a lunatic joy: Lily Tomlin, George Carlin, Robin Williams, Nathan Lane, Rosie O'Donnell, Shirley MacLaine, Barry Manilow, Gil Cates, Steve Martin, Oscar's own Billy Crystal, and from the very beginning, Kaye Ballard.

I am fond of saying that on *Hollywood Squares* I sat to the left of Whoopi Goldberg . . . if that's possible. There has never been anyone quite like Whoopi, for all the reasons you know and for a dozen more I have been privileged to discover. She was in a square for a while, but she has been in my corner forever. (And anyone who knows her knows there is no Whoopi without Tom Leonardis.)

And two extraordinary women:

The bravest person I know, Joan Hyler.

And my constant source of inspiration for over fifty years, and if you read that in the voice of Sophie Tucker it will sound like a much bigger deal than it is—wait a minute, it *is* a big fucking deal!—the woman who changed my life before she changed yours, the Divine Miss M . . . Bette Midler.

No one can follow her.

Index

Page numbers in italics indicate photographs

ABC, 58, 64, 75, 158–159, 180
Abercrombie, Ian, 95
Academy Awards. *See* 61st Academy
    Awards
Academy of Motion Pictures Arts and
    Sciences, 171, 173, 178, 179,
    180
Acuña, Jason "Wee Man," 45n
Adams, Lee, 42
Adams, Oleta, 173
Adelman, Sybil, 159
Adelson, Merv, 164
Ain't Misbehavin' (stage musical), 127
"Alabama Song, The," 29
Albertson, Jack, 35
Albrecht, Howard, 39
All in the Family, 27
Allen, Debbie, 117
Allen, Joe, 142–143, 150, 182
Allen, Peter, 135
Allen, Woody, 12n, 35, 89
Amanda's, 26n
Anderson, Eddie "Rochester," 66n
Anderson, Judith, 44, 95
Anderson, Louie, 152, 153, 154
André, Eric, 184

Andrews, Julie, 13, 53, 115
Ann-Margret, 104, 116
Archerd, Army, 117, 177
Archerd, Selma, 117
Armisen, Fred, 185
Around the World in 80 Days (1956),
    104n
Arthur, Bea, 25–26, 26n, 28–29, 165
Astaire, Fred, 13
Atami, Japan, 151–152, 155
Attichitcuk (character), 15, 19
awards shows. *See* 61st Academy
    Awards; *Look of the Year, The*
    (1988)
Ayers-Allen, Phylicia, 117, 118
Aykroyd, Dan, 19

B movies, 8, 10
Bacall, Lauren, 116, 124
Bagdad Cafe (1987), 173
Baker, Josephine, 118
Bakker, Tammy Faye, 184
Baldwin, Alec, 170
Ball, Lucille, 172, 173
Ballard, Kaye, 148
Ballroom (stage musical), 138

Barbara Mandrell & the Mandrell Sisters,
6
Barefoot in the Park (play), 73
Baretta, 92
Barnes, Billy, 40, 42
Barron, Jeffrey, 160–161
Barty, Billy, 44–46, 50, 56
Batman (1960s TV series), 45
Battle of the Network Stars, 14
Beach Blanket Babylon (stage musical),
174–175
Beacham, Stephanie, 152
Beaches (1988), 176
Beatty, Warren, 66
Beaumont, Binkie, 76–77
Beauty and the Beast (TV series), 92
Begelman, David, 84–85, 87
Behar, Joy, 148, 149, 150
Belolo, Henri, 105, 106
Bennett, Michael, 138
Benny, Jack, 66, 66n, 159
Bergen, Candice, 179
Bergen, Edgar, 75
Berle, Milton, 75, 77–78
Berle, Ruth, 78
Berlin, Irving, 166
Bernstein, Ira, 54
Best Original Song (Academy Awards),
172–173
"Beth," 57
Beverly Hillbillies, The, 27
Bewitched, 34
Bialik, Mayim, 176
Birdland, Los Angeles, 165
Bisset, Jacqueline "Jackie," 104,
106–107, 179
Blake, Robert, 92
Bluestein, Steve, 67
Bob Newhart Show, The, 27
Boba Fett (character), 22–23
Bono, Sonny, 7, 62, 113
Booker, Bob, 39–40, 159
Bowman, Eileen, 176, 177

Brady, Carol (character). *See* Henderson,
Florence
Brady Bunch, The, 63–64
Brady Bunch Hour, The, 63–80
cast expectations of, 72–73, 78
executive producers of, 66
guest stars on, 75–76
premise of, 65–66
press reviews of, 79
production schedule for, 80
Rip Taylor role in, 71–72
scheduling, 80
show within the show, 65, 70–71
storylines, 76–77
writer's room for, 66–70
Brady Bunch Movie, The (1995), 80
Brady family
sequels, 80
as variety performers, 64–65, 71
Bravo (cable channel), 184, 187–188
BravoCon, 188
Brecht, Bertolt, 25, 29
Broadway Street, Los Angeles, 96–97
Brooks, Mel, 102
Brown, Barry, 130
Browne, Coral, 76–77
Bulletin (Philadelphia), 132
Burke, Billie, 47
Burnett, Carol, 62, 63, 71
Burns, George, 6, 64
Butch Cassidy and the Sundance Kid
(1969), 84
Butthole Surfers, 129
Bye Bye Birdie, 34, 35, 42
Byrne, Joe, 40

CAA (Creative Artists Agency), 68
cable television, 5
Caesar, Sid, 6
Caine, Michael, 171
CalArts (California Institute of the
Arts), 96
Call Me Madam, 114

Cameron, James, 83
Campbell, Joseph, 8
Can't Stop the Music (1980), 103–108, 111–115, 116–119
Canutt, Yakima, 170
Capp, Al, 43
Captain & Tenille, the, 63
Carkoon, 26–27
Carmen Miranda costume, 73–74
Carney, Art, 17, 17n, 19, 21, 24
Carol Burnett Show, The, 17–18, 29, 62
Carpenters, the, 126
Carr, Allan, 103–106, 107–108, 110, 120, 180–181
    Can't Stop the Music and, 112–118
    firing of Vilanch over money, 116
    61st Academy Awards and, 171–177
    weight issues of, 108–109
Carradine, John, 92–93
Carrie (stage musical), 97
Carroll, Diahann, 20
Carson, Rubin, 159–160
Carter, Lynda, 6
Cassidy, David, 64
Cassidy, Shaun, 80
Cates, Gilbert "Gil," 181, 182
Catskills on Broadway (stage show), 145–146
Catwoman (character), 45
Cavalcade (1933), 13n
Caveman (1981), 91
CBS, 6, 9–10, 12–13, 27, 167
Channing, Carol, 164–167
"Chanson D'Amour," 62
Charisse, Cyd, 177
Charles, Ray, 58n
Charo, 73n, 75, 157–160, *160*, 161–163
Charo, 159–163
Charo and the Sergeant, 158
Chase, Chevy, 38
Chasen's (restaurant), 165
Chef Gormaanda (character), 17–18

Cher, 7, 19–20, 49, 62, 112–114, 115
Chevrolet, 180
Chewbacca, 12n, 14, 92
Child, Julia, 19
Cinema Chien, 119
Clams on the Half Shell Revue (stage show), 125, 130
claque, the, 137, 142
Clark, Petula, 23
Cleese, John, 26n
Clone Wars, The, 95
Close Encounters of the Third Kind (1977), 9
Coco, James "Jimmy," 109, 111
Cocoanut Grove set, 175–176, 177
Cohen, Alexander H., 145–150
Cohen, Andy, 188
Cohen, Claudia, 38
Colbert, Stephen, 139, 185
Collins, Phil, 172, 173
Colt, Alvin, 149
Columbo, 80
Comedy Tonight (stage show), 149–150.
    See also *Three* (stage show)
competition shows, 6–7, 14. See also *Look of the Year, The* (1988)
Connery, Sean, 171
Connors, Mike, 161–162, 163
"Convoy," 48
Conway, Tim, 49, 49n, 50, 55, 62
Coogan, Keith, 173
Cooper, Alice, 42, 122
Copperfield, David, 6, 152, 153
Coppola, Francis Ford, 23
Corden, James, 185
Core, Natalie, 95
Costner, Kevin, 83
Coward, Noël, 13, 13n, 40, 54
Cox, Richard, 128–129, 132, *136*, 139, 141
Crane, Harry, 161
Crawford, Christina, 132n
Crawford, Joan, 133

Crazy Horse, Paris, 105
Creative Artists Agency (CAA), 68
Criss, Peter, 57
Crosby, Mary Frances, 90, 101
cross-plugging, 14
Cruising (1980), 128–129
Crystal, Billy, 170, 179, 182
Cugat, Xavier "Coogie," 158
Cummings, Bob, 70
Cuntface, 27, 28–29
Curry, Tim, 51, 187

Dakota (apartment building), 36n
Daley, Richard J., 77
Dalí, Salvador, 158
Dallas, 90
Dame Edna Everage (character), 130n
Dan Danger (character), 127, 128
Dan Tana (restaurant), 85
Danza, Tony, 127
Dart, Iris Rainer. *See* Rainer, Iris
Davidson, Bing, 38
Davis, Ann B., 70–72
Davis, Bette, 128
Davis, Clive, 126
Davis, Geena, 171, 179
Davis, Michael, 146, 150
Davis, Sammy, Jr., 171
Dayan, Assaf "Assi," 89
De Mornay, Rebecca, 132
De Vol, Frank, 162
Deep Throat (1972), 50n
Deer Hunter, The (1978), 172
del Toro, Guillermo, 83, 92
DeMille, Cecil B., 127
Dempsey, Patrick, 174
Dent, Bucky, 139
"Diamonds Are a Girl's Best Friend," 165
Diller, Barry, 137, 137n, 141
Disco Demolition Night, 119–120
"Disco Lady," 58–59
Discoland: Where the Music Never Stops.
    See *Can't Stop the Music* (1980)

Disney, Walt, 96
Disney's Hollywood Studios, 179–180
Doda, Carol, 175n
Dogpatch, USA, 44n
Don Kirshner's Rock Concert, 104, 105,
    106
Donny & Marie, 1–2, 35, 36, 68
Doors, the, 29
Dopey (character), 28
Dore, Bonny, 75
Dragon, Daryl "the Captain," 63
Drai, Victor, 104–105, 106–107
Drai's (restaurant), 105
Duke, Patty, 21
Duke University, 109
Dunaway, Faye, 115, 132n

Eastwood, Clint, 150
Ebb, Fred, 146, 149, 174
Ed Sullivan Theater, 139
Eden, Barbara, 27
Eder, Richard, 141
Edsel, the, 121
Eisenhower Theater (Kennedy Center),
    134
Eisner, Michael, 137
El Capitan Theatre, Los Angeles, 119
Elephant Walk (1954), 111
Elite (modeling agency), 151
EMI, 113
Empire Strikes Back, The (1980), 9
Empty Nest, 14
Endangered Species (1982), 85–86
Ethel Merman Disco Album, The, 139
Evans, Dale, 177
Everage, Dame Edna (character), 130n
Ewing, J. R. (character), 90

Fallon, Jimmy, 185
Fawlty Towers, 26n
Faye, Alice, 42n, 177
Feldman, Corey, 174
Fett, Boba (character), 22–23

Fiddler on the Roof (stage musical), 25
Fink's Mules, 64
First Family, The (album), 39
First Monday in October (play), 138
Fisher, Carrie, 11, 21, 27, 31, 179
Fisher, Eddie, 173
Fisher, Joely, 173
Fisher, Tricia Leigh, 173
Flaming Snot, 129–130
Follies (stage musical), 137
Fonda, Henry, 114
Ford, Harrison, 16
Ford Motor Company, 13
Foreman, John, 84–90, 99–100, 101, 102
Fosse, Bob, 117
Foster, George, 39–40, 159
Four Musketeers, The (1974), 115
Francis, Arlene, 135
Francks, Don, 23
Frankie Bradley's (restaurant), 131
Freeman, Damita Jo, 127
Friedkin, William, 128
Friedman, Gary William, 122, 124
Frog Lady. *See* Lewis, Marcia

Gabel, Martin, 135
Gallagher, Barbara, 159
Garavani, Valentino, 54n
Garland, Judy, 13, 84, 186
Gavilan, 85
Geffen, David, 126
Gelbart, Larry, 132
Gentlemen Prefer Blondes (1949), 166
Get Bruce (1999), 185, 185n
Gilligan's Island, 69
Girl Can't Help It, The (1956), 4n
Gleason, Jackie, 6, 17n
Gloomsbury Manor, 43, 56
Glover, Savion, 174
Godzilla, 68
Goldblum, Jeff, 171
Golden Girls, The, 14, 163–164

Gong Show, The, 71
Gopnik, Adam, 142
Gore, Altovise, 118
Gormaanda, Chef (character), 17–18
Graham, Ronny, 38, 67, 75, 79
Grean, Robin, 127
Grease (1978), 9, 104, 107, 113
Great Pit of Carkoon, 26–27
Green, Al, 74
Green Acres, 27
Greenwich Village, 117, 119
Griffin, Merv, 139, 176, 177
Griffith, Melanie, 171, 178–179
Grimes, Tammy, 112, 120
Guttenberg, Steve, 116–117

Hackett, Buddy, 111
Hagman, Larry, 13n
Hairspray (stage musical), *186*
Halliday, Lila (character), 127, 128, 131
Hamilton, Ashley, 152
Hamilton, Carrie, 173
Hamilton, George, 6, 152, 152n, 153, 154
Hamilton, Margaret, 37, 40, 42–43, 44
Hamlisch, Marvin, 172, 174
Hardy Boys, The, 80
Hargitay, Mickey, 4n
Harlettes, 127
Harris, Susan, 163–164
Hart, Terry, 67
Hauser, Wings, 128
Havoc, June, 117
Hawn, Goldie, 179
Hayes, Billie, 43–44, 66
Hayman, Fred, 171
Hayworth, Rita, 123
HBO, 5
Hearst, William Randolph, 112
Heatherton, Joey and Ray, 6–7
Hee Haw, 27
Hellboy (2004), 92
Hellinger, Mark, 136

Hellinger Theatre, 135–136
Hello, Dolly!, 164, 166
Henderson, Florence, 53–57, 63–64, 65, 72, 78–79, *78*
Henne (proposed TV series), 166–167
Henry Miller's Theatre, 140
Hepburn, Katharine, 85, 109
Herbert, Frank, 8
Heston, Charlton, 127
High Risk (1981), 87
Hines, Gregory, 171
Hocus Pocus (1993), 60
Hoff, Ashley, 132n
Hollywood Paramount, 119
Hollywood Squares, 34, 59, 130n, 184, 186
Holt, Courtney, 126
Holt, Fritz, 130
Holt, Will, 122–123, 124, 126, 132
Hope, Bob, 3–4, 160, 172, 173
H.R. Pufnstuf, 43
Hudson, Rock, 107
Humphries, Barry, 130n
Hurricane Saturday, 14
Huston, Angelica, 89–90, 102
Huston, John, 90, 102

I Dream of Jeannie, 27
"I Wanna Be an Oscar Winner," 174
Ice Pirates, The (1984), 87–102
    casting for, 89–95
    filming of, 95–102
    The Water Planet reworked to become, 87–88
Imperial Hotel, Tokyo, 153
Inge, William, 123
Inn Trigue (Washington, DC), 135
Inquirer (Philadelphia), 132
Irene (stage musical), 21
Irma (taco truck lady), 159
Itchy (character), 15, 19
"I've Got a Lovely Bunch of Coconuts," 176

Jabba the Hut, 26–27
Jackson, Michael, 152
Jamie (*Platinum* character), 124, 132
Japan, 151–152, 154
Jefferson Starship, 10, 22
Jenner, Bruce, 114–115
Jenner, Caitlyn. *See* Jenner, Bruce
John Davidson Show, The, 163
Johnson, Don, 171, 178–179
Johnson, Van, 91
Jonah, Dolly, 122, 126
Jones, Shirley, 64

Kael, Pauline, 50n
Kaelin, Kato, 185
Kagan, Mike, 67
Kander, John, 146, 149, 174
Kashyyyk, 14
Kaye, Danny, 13
Kellman, Barnet, 165, 166, 167
Kelly, Gene, 108
Kelly, Roz, 49
Kennedy Center, Washington, DC, 134
Kerkorian, Kirk, 101–102
Kerr, Deborah, 135
keyboard warfare, 18, 20, 31–32, 55n, 169
"Kids," 34, 42
Kimmel, Jimmy, 185
King, Stephen, 97
"King of the Nighttime World," 57
KISS, 51–52, 51n–52n, 57–58
Kitt, Eartha, 136
Kleinschmitt, Carl, 67, 69
Knoxville, Johnny, 45
Korman, Harvey, 17–18, 17n, 24, 26, 26n, 62
Krauss, Marvin, 129
Krofft, Marty, 43, 45, 58, 66, 68
Krofft, Sid, 43, 45, 58, 66
Krofftettes, 75
Krull (1983), 84

Kubelsky, Benjamin. *See* Benny, Jack
Kuehn, Andrew, 185n

La Russo, Louis, II, 122–123, 124, 125
Lake, Ricki, 174
Lamour, Dorothy, 177
Lamppost Reunion (play), 124
Lancaster, Burt, 85
Lane, Abbe, 158
Lansbury, Angela, 124
Lattanzi, Matt, 174
Laugh-In, 128
Laurel Canyon, 93–94
Law & Order, 186
Lawrence, Jerome "Jerry," 138–139, *138*
Lawrence, Vicki, 62
Layton, Joe, 20, 125–126, 127, 128,
    129, 130, 131, 141, 142
Lazar, Irving "Swifty," 180
Lee, Lorelei (character), 166
Leff, Jeff (character), 126–127, 128,
    132
Legend of Walks Far Woman, The (1982),
    116
Leia, Princess (character), 21, 31
Lemmon, Jack, 172
Lennon, John, 36n
Les Poupées de Paris (stage show), 43
Lester, Richard, 115
"Let's Stay Together," 74
Levi, Dolly (character), 166
Lewis, Marcia, 93–95, 99
Lidsville, 43
Life Day, 14–15, 30–31
Life with Elizabeth, 46
Li'l Abner (cartoon strip), 43, 44n
Li'l Abner (stage musical), 44, 46
"Little Drummer Boy," 11
Look of the Year, The (1988), 151
Look What's Happened to Rosemary's Baby
    (1976), 36
Lorimar, 164, 167
Los Angeles Theatre, 96–97, 98–99

Loudon, Dorothy, 146, 147, 148–149,
    150
Love and Death (1975), 89
Love Boat, The, 158
Lovelace, Linda, 50n
Lover Come Back (1961), 107
Lowe, Chad, 173
Lowe, Charles, 164–165, 166, 167
Lowe, Rob, 176, 178, 181
Lucas, George, 10–11, 14, 19, 26–27
Lucasfilm, 10
Lucky Liz (airplane), 104n
Lumpawarrump "Lumpy" (character),
    15, 22–24
Lynde, Paul, 33–37, 38, 41–42, 48, 52,
    54–55, 56, 59–60. See also *Paul
    Lynde Halloween Special, The*

MacDonald, Jeanette, 175n
"Macho Man," 105
Mackie, Bob, 18, 131, 185
magic shows, 6
Makowsky, Zelda, 77
Mallatobuck "Malla" (character), 15–16,
    17, 21, 22, 30
Mammy Yokum (character), 43
Manard, Biff, 39
Mandalorian, The, 14–15
Manhattan Transfer, 61–63
Manimal, 92
Mansfield, Jayne, 4n
Margolis, Jeff, 171–172
Mark Hellinger Theatre, 135–136
Mark Twain Prize broadcasts, 134
Martin, Judith, 134
Martin, Mary, 13, 13n
Martin, Steve, 38, 170
Mary Tyler Moore Show, The, 27
M*A*S*H, 27
Matthau, Walter, 17n, 172
Matuszak, John "Tooz," 91
McClanahan, Rue, 46
McCormick, Maureen, 64

McCormick, Pat, 87n
McLuhan, Marshall, 40–41
Me Nobody Knows, The (stage musical), 122
Meet Me at the Melba (Woodard), 105
Menefee, Pete, 74
Merman, Ethel, 114, 122, 139
Merrick, David, *138*, 145
Merv Griffin Show, The, 139
Metro-Goldwyn-Mayer (MGM) TV division, 85
Meyers, Seth, 185
Middle Age Crazy (1980), 67
Midler, Bette, 29, 60, 125–126
Midnight in the Garden of Good and Evil (1997), 150
"Milk Shake," 108
Miranda, Carmen, 73, 73n
Mitchell, Joni, 21
Mommie Dearest (Crawford), 132, 132n
Mommie Dearest (proposed stage musical), 100
Monroe, Marilyn, 4n, 66n, 77–78, 166
Moore, Demi, 179
Moore, Roger, 171
Morali, Jacques, 105, 117, 120
Mordente, Lisa, 125, 132, *136*, 139
Mordente, Tony, 125
Mother Teresa, 107
Mr. Dirt (character), 38
MTV, 5n
Mungle, Matthew, 97–98
My Fair Lady (stage musical), 136
My 600-Lb. Life, 111

Nancy Drew, 80
Nash, N. Richard, 85
NBC, 5, 80, 188
Nederlander, Gladys Rackmil "Gladdie," 129–130, 142
Nederlander, Robert, 142
Nelson, Tracy, 173
nepo-baby productions, 173

Netflix, 119
Nettleton, Lois, 85
New Faces (stage show), 38
New York Times, 141
New Yorker, 141
Newman, Paul, 47, 84, 100
Newman-Foreman, 84
Newmar, Julie, 45–46
Newton, Wayne, 6
Newton-John, Olivia, 107, 113, 174
Nicholas, Fayard, 176
Nicholas, Harold, 176
Nick at Nite, 80
Noises Off (play), 146
Nolte, Nick, 91
North Bridgton, ME, 126
North Dallas Forty (1979), 91
Norton, Ed (character), 17n
Norton, Edward, 17n
Not Ready for Prime Time Players, the, 5
Novak, Kim, 171, 175n, 179
Nurses, 14
Nype, Russell, 114

O'Brien, Conan, 185
Odd Couple (play), 17n
O'Donnell, Rosie, 116
Oklahoma! (stage musical), 125
Once Is Not Enough (1975), 124
Once Upon a Mattress (stage musical), 71
O'Neal, Patrick, 173
Opera House (Kennedy Center), 134
Oscar Wars (Schulman), 176
Oscars, the. *See* 61st Academy Awards
Osmond, Donny and Marie, 6, 7, 42, 68
　　double for Marie, 68–69
　　See also *Donny & Marie*
Osmonds, the, 11, 35, 68, 75
O'Toole, Peter, 54, 54n
Ovitz, Mike, 67–68, 69

Paramount, 80, 124, 125, 127, 140, 142

Paramount Theater, Los Angeles, 119

Paris, Norman, 147

Parker, Corey, 174

Parks, Hildy, 146, 171, 176

Partridge Family, The, 64

Paul Lynde Comedy Hour, The, 35

Paul Lynde Halloween Special, The, 36–59

    ABC censors and, 59

    finale, 58–59

    Lynde characters in, 36, 48–49, 53–55, 56

    musical interludes in, 42, 50, 51, 56–58

    storyline for, 36–37, 40–41, 42–45, 46, 47, 53, 56–57

    writers for, 38–40

Peacock (streaming service), 188

Pearlman, Ronny, 38–39

Perelman, Ronald, 38

Perlman, Ron, 38, 91–92

Perrine, Valerie, 117

Philadelphia Bulletin, 132

Philadelphia Inquirer, 132

Pickles (dog), 77

Pierce, David Hyde, 187

Pippin (stage musical), 140

Platinum (stage musical), 121–144

    casting of, 125, 128–129

    commercial filmed for, 140

    early New York previews of, 137–138

    final rehearsal run-through, 129

    morphing of *Sunset* into, 125–130

    opening night in New York, 140–142

    original concept for, 121–125

    out-of-town tryouts, 130–135

    reviews for, 130–132, 134, 141

    run length of, 142

    set design, 127, 131

    See also *Sunset* (stage musical)

podcasts, 1

Pointer Sisters, 6, 152–153, 154

Poupées de Paris, Les (stage show), 43

Power, Tyrone, Jr., 173

Price, Vincent, 75–77

Prince, Harold "Hal," 123

Prizzi's Honor (1985), 90, 102

programming wheels, 79–80

"Proud Mary," 178

Queen Mary (ship), 131

Quest for Fire (1981), 91–92

Rackmil, Gladys "Gladdie." *See* Nederlander, Gladys Rackmil "Gladdie"

Raffill, Stewart, 87–88, 96, 100

Rainer, Iris, 159

Rainmaker, The (play), 85

Randall, Tony, 6

Rashad, Ahmad, 118

Rashad, Phylicia, 118. *See also* Ayers-Allen, Phylicia

Raye, Martha, 121

Redford, Robert, 73

Reed, Robert, 64–65, 72–74, 78

Reeve, Christopher "Chris," 9, 114

Reinking, Ann, 173

Reynolds, Burt, 85

Reynolds, Debbie, 21, 187

Rhinestone Trucker, 48–49

Rice House, 109–111

Richie, Lionel, 126

Ridley, Daisy, 15

Rivera, Chita, 125

Roberts, Doris, 109–110, 111

Roberts, Michael D., 92, 95, 97, 98

Robinson, Bill "Bojangles," 176

Robinson, Holly, 174

Rocky Horror Picture Show, The (1975), 51

Rodriguez, Guillermo, 185

Rogers, Roy, 177

Ronstadt, Linda, 38–39

Roppongi, Tokyo, 154
Roseland, 140
Rosemary's Baby (1968), 36n
Ross, Diana, 118, 126
Roth, Lynn, 159, 163, 164, 165–166
Rowan and Martin, 6
Rush, Barbara, 117
Russell, Kurt, 179
Russell, Rosalind, 123, 125

Sahl, Mort, 146, 148, 149, 150
Santa Barbara, 95
Schulman, Michael, 176
Schwartz, Sherwood, 69–70
Screen Actors Guild, 186
Seawell, Wallace, 165
Segovia, Andrés, 157
Semmelweis (play), 134
Sheehan, Kitty, 77
Sherman, Stanford, 84
Shore, Dinah, 6
Short, Martin, 179
Shubert Theatre, Philadelphia, 130
Siegfried & Roy, 126
Sills, Beverly, 139
Silver, Jo, 174
Silver, Steve, 174, 175, 177
Silverman, Fred, 35, 61–62, 64, 70,
    159
Simmons, Gene, 52
Simon, Carly, 172, 173
Simon, Neil, 73, 129
Simpson, Ray, 118
61st Academy Awards, 169, 171–179
Skid Row. *See* Broadway Street, Los
    Angeles
Skywalker, Luke (character), 16
Slater, Christian, 174
Slick, Grace, 22
Smith, Alexis, 122–124, 128, 129, 131,
    132–133, 135, 136, 137, 139
Smothers, Tom "Tommy" and Dick
    "Dickie," 27n

Smothers Brothers Comedy Hour, The,
    27, 27n
Snavely, 26n
Snow White (character), 180
Snow White Cafe, 180
Snow White show, 171, 175–181
social media. *See* keyboard warfare
Sokol, Marilyn, 112, 120
Sommers, Avery, 127
Son of Sam, the, 8n
Sondheim, Stephen, 123, 124
Song of Norway (1970), 54
Sonny & Cher, 6. *See also* Bono, Sonny;
    Cher
Sons of Anarchy, 92
Space Herpe, 99
Spaceballs (1987), 102
specials, TV. *See* TV specials
sponsors, 36, 50–51
Springfield, Rick, 128
Stage 30, 93, 101, 102
Star Is Born, A (1976), 127
Star Wars (1977), 8–9
Star Wars Holiday Special, The, 8–31
    alien scenes in, 28–29
    Cantina scene in, 24–27, 28
    cartoon of Boba Fett in, 22–23
    CBS censors and, 27
    holograms in, 22
    musical interludes in, 19–20,
        29–30
    offer to Vilanch to write, 5
    origin of, 8–12
    reactions to, 31
    storyline for, 14–19, 21–24, 30–31
Starr, Ringo, 52n, 91
Steel Pier (stage musical), 116
Stevens, Craig, 123, 133
Stewart, James "Jimmy," 171, 179
Streep, Meryl, 54n
Streisand, Barbra, 13, 87n, 166
Stritch, Elaine, 122, 163
Strouse, Charles, 42

Structure House, Durham, NC, 109, 110
subtitles, use of, 12–13, 12n
Sues, Alan, 128
Sukarno, Dewi, 4n
Sullivan, Ed, 16n–17n, 34
Summer Brave (play), 123
Sunday Mystery Movie (NBC), 80
Sunset (stage musical), 121–127. See also *Platinum* (stage musical)
Sunset Blvd. (1950), 124
Sunset Boulevard billboard, 119
Swayze, Patrick, 179
Sweeney Todd (stage musical), 124
sweeps, 5, 13–14

Taking My Turn (stage musical), 122
Taylor, Rip, 71–72, 73, 76, 77
team hosting, of variety shows, 6, 62
Television Academy, 170
Telson, Bob, 173
Tennille, Toni, 63, 74
Terry, Phillip, 133
Thoroughly Modern Millie (1967), 166
"Those Were the Days," 29
Three (stage show), 146–150. See also *Comedy Tonight* (stage show)
Threepenny Opera, The (play), 25
Tilton, Charlene, 14
Times Square Church. *See* Mark Hellinger Theatre
Todd, Mike, 104n
Tomlin, Lily, 178
Tony Orlando & Dawn, 6
Transfer, the. *See* Manhattan Transfer
truck culture, 48
Tune, Tommy, 122–123
Turner, Ike, 74
Turner, Lana, 123
Turner, Ted, 102
Turner, Tina, 74–75
Tuscadero, Pinky (character), 49

"Tuxedo Junction," 62
TV specials, 5–6, 13–14, 35, 40n. *See also* 61st Academy Awards; *Paul Lynde Halloween Special, The*; *Star Wars Holiday Special, The*
20th Century-Fox, 4n

Uncle Arthur (character), 34
Urich, Heather, 85
Urich, Robert "Bob," 85–86, 88, 92, 95, 98

vagina imagery, in *Star Wars*, 26–27
Valenti, Jack, 179
Valentino, Rudolph, 54n
Vanity Fair party, 180
variety show format, 5–8, 13–14, 58, 62, 63. See also *Brady Bunch Hour, The*; TV specials
Vega$, 85
Vernon, Jackie, 59
Vilanch, Bruce
    on actors' gender identity and their roles, 55, 55n
    on answering phones, 4
    awards won by, 151, 170, *170*
    on bad ideas, 121
    on being a joke writer, 3–4
    on being mascot characters, 28
    on being too hip, 63
    career reflection by, 1–2
    critique of *Platinum* by, 141
    on drug use in the 1970s, 11
    at the fat farm, 109–112
    on finales, 58
    firing from *Can't Stop the Music*, 116–117
    in Japan, 151–152, 154–155
    late-night talk show pilot hosted by, 183–188
    on making script changes while on the road, 134–135
    Marcia Lewis and, 93–94

on Philadelphia as a review town,
    130–132
photographs of, *94*, *136*, *160*, *186*
on pleasing sponsors, 50–51
remark made to *Platinum* audience
    member, 139
on taking breaks at the Paramount
    lot, 127–128
as Weird Wendon, 87–88, 97–98,
    99, 102
work on awards show done by, 170
on writing for television, 5–7
Vilanch, Henne, 77, 78, 161, 166–167,
    185–187, *186*, 188
Village People, 104, 105–106, 107,
    113–114, 117, 120
virtual reality helmets, 19
von Furstenberg, Betsy, 137
von Furstenberg, Diane, 137, 137n

Walk with Love and Death, A (1969), 89
Walker, Nancy, 35, 110, 113, 118
Walt Disney Company, 181
Walt Disney World, 180
Walters, Barbara, 164
Warner Bros., 133, 136
Water Planet, The, 83–86. See also *Ice
    Pirates, The* (1984)
Webber, Andrew Lloyd, 124
Weill, Kurt, 25
Weinstein, Harvey, 185n
Weinstein, Sol, 39
Welch, Ken and Mitzie, 29
Welch, Raquel, 6, 115–116
Wells, Frank, 179–180
Wendon, Emperor "Weird" (character),
    87–88, 97–98, 99, 102
Westinghouse, Lady (character), 54
What's Up, Tiger Lily? (1966), 12n–13n
Wheeler, Hugh, 124

wheels, programming, 79–80
White, Betty, 46–47, 165
Will Success Spoil Rock Hunter? (1957),
    4n
Williams, Barry, 64
Williams, Esther, 75n
Williams, Paul, 87, 87n, 88
Williams, Robin, 185, 185n
Willis, Bruce, 179
Willis, Victor, 106, 117–118
Winning (1969), 84
Witchiepoo, Wilhelmina W. (character),
    43–44, 66
With Love, Mommie Dearest (Hoff),
    132n
Wolf, Richard Anthony "Dick," 14
Wolfman Jack, 48
Women, The (play), 123
Wonderful Town (stage musical), 125
Woodard, Bronté, 105, 106, 107–108,
    109–111, 114, 120
Woodward, Joanne, 84, 100
Wookiees, 12–13, 12n
World of Wonder, 184
writers and writers' rooms, 37–40, 58,
    66–70, 159–161. *See also specific
    writers*
Wynn, Tracy Keenan, 94

Xanadu (1980), 108
Xenon (disco), 140

Yablans, Frank, 100, 101
Yakuza, 154
"Yes We Can Can," 153
Yokum, Mammy (character), 43
Youngman, Henny, 161

Zappa, Frank, 95
Zeffirelli, Franco, 89